Teaching Literature as Reflective Practice

Teaching Literature as Reflective Practice

Kathleen Blake Yancey
Clemson University

National Council of Teachers of English
1111 W. Kenyon Road, Urbana, Illinois 61801-1096

Staff Editor: Bonny Graham

Interior Design: Doug Burnett

Cover Design: Barbara Yale-Read

NCTE Stock Number: 51167

Every effort has been made to provide current URLs and e-mail addresses, but because of the rapidly changing nature of the Web, some sites and addresses may no longer be accessible.

Library of Congress Cataloging-in-Publication Data

Yancey, Kathleen Blake, 1950–
　　Teaching literature as reflective practice / Kathleen Blake Yancey.
　　　　p. cm.
　　Includes bibliographical references and index.
　　ISBN 0-8141-5116-7 (pbk)
　1. English philology—Study and teaching (Higher)—United States.
2. Literature—Study and teaching (Higher)—United States. I. Title.
　　PE68 . U5Y36 2004
　　807' . 1'173—dc22

2004006586

Permission Acknowledgments

Contents

Preface

I went into education in large part to change the world through reading and writing. It is through reading and writing that we compose both self and community, that we learn to understand the other and value that difference. This is the commitment we make: to learn how to do this in a way that balances both text and person, that understands text as operating at the intersection of media and genre, that raises questions and possibility as it fosters a public reader.

This book is an effort to articulate how I constructed the task (and why I construct it as I do), what happened in the process, and what this means for 95 percent of postsecondary students—that is, for our students who do *not* major in English, but who represent our hopes for a reading public.

Writing this book has been a pleasure, and I have many to thank for making it so. My students, whose readings continue to challenge, frustrate, amuse, surprise, and inspire me. The colleagues on the College Section of NCTE who encouraged this work, especially Geoff Sirc and Jeanne Gunner. The many friends and colleagues who workshopped much of this material with me, particularly the teachers working with Mary Kay Crouch at California State University, Fullerton; with Jeannette Gibson at Georgia Perimeter College; with Susan Greene at Greenville Tech; and with Joyce Neff at Old Dominion University. I've been in partnership with teachers at Virginia Beach City Schools and Tidewater Community College for six years, and to them I owe a special debt: Elizabeth Beagle, Jane Hunn, Chris Jennings, Lisa Long, Lizette Picello, Lorna Roberson, and Fran Sharer.

Thanks also to my writing group at Clemson—Teddi Fishman, Morgan Gresham, Michael Neal, and Summer Smith—who help me laugh and help me write. To Art Young, who first shared the value of not-understanding: thanks. To Karen Schiff, whose fascination with the connect between poetry and life encouraged mine: thanks as well. To Bud Weiser, a thanks for thinking that the proposal for this volume had merit, and to Joe Janangelo, for providing a sympathetic reading and a critical eye both.

Not least, thanks to David, Genevieve, and Matthew, who continue to read with and against me.

Kathleen Blake Yancey
Clemson, South Carolina

1 Teaching Literature as Reflective Practice: Context, Vocabulary, Curriculum

I was of three minds,
Like a tree
In which there are three blackbirds

Wallace Stevens, "Thirteen Ways
of Looking at a Blackbird"

I want to begin this chapter, and this book, with a set of five observations that collectively speak to learning, literacy, and schooling.

Observation One. At least once a year, I teach a general education literature course, the course that literally is the last course in literature most students will complete. In teaching this course—which the catalog copy tells students is "Forms of Literature," focusing on the genres of poetry, novel, and drama—I ask students to think about the reading of literature as well as the reading of other texts. To introduce this "reading process" framework to students, I ask a fundamental kind of question: "How is reading e. e. cummings different from reading your calculus textbook?" The hope is that for the students these texts invite different reading processes; the reality is that too often they don't. When I teach a different kind of course, one in which the reading is less like poetry and more like that of calculus—say a course in rhetorical theory—I get a similar reaction. For most students, reading is a unified construct, and I continue to have a vague sense—akin, I think, to what Freud called "dis-ease"—that the writing and reading tasks I assign *in* school aren't the same kinds of reading and writing that students do *outside* of school. And what students *do* outside of class: it's not making its way into my classroom either. This, I think, is a problem. *I agree.*

———

Portions of this chapter appeared in, or were adapted from, Kathleen Yancey's *Reflection in the Writing Classroom*, copyright 1998 Utah State University Press. Used by permission.

Observation Two. I know what the numbers say about what students are doing outside of class: "The average American child," we're told, "spends 78 minutes a week reading, 102 minutes a week on homework and study, and 12 hours a week watching television. . . ." I also know that new forms of literacy seem to proliferate more quickly than we can track them, and that many of them invite sophisticated forms of learning. James Paul Gee (*What Video*), for instance, has documented new genres of literacy that children acquire through playing video games, and the same logic is apparently generalizable since the military is now using video games for leadership training. Oprah Book Club selections make new celebrities—and spark ersatz literary scandals, as we saw in the case of Jonathan Franzen, author of *The Corrections* (who refused the designation and then apologized). Poetry jams have morphed from urban corners to rural campuses; at both sites, they are what Deborah Brandt calls "self-sponsored literacy events." In another case of self-sponsorship, readers note their book preferences on Amazon.com's Listmania and then provide commentary on blogs and wikis. Functioning largely *outside* of school, these literacies seem quite successful, if measured by the social goals people meet day in and day out.

Observation Three. When I go to a movie with people I like whose educational experiences and values are similar to my own—my husband (an engineer turned Web guy) and daughter (a double major in psychology and biology) and son (a double major in engineering and math)—I find that we haven't even seen the same movie, much less responded to it the same way.

> Ideally, we want students to have the opportunity to cultivate an attitude—intellectual and social—that is at once playful and responsible. It is playful in its willingness to examine ideas, to imagine different worlds, to resist habits of thought and social conventions; it is responsible in its fundamental connections to the world.—Nancy Cantor and Steven Schomberg

Observation Four. One of the big shifts in higher education, as in K–12, is a move away from the sage-on-the-stage, teacher-centered, lecture-driven model of teaching to a learner-centered, interactive model. Another shift involves understanding school learning as a "re-mediated" learning of the kind we first associate with toddlers. This new college learning, like that of young children, is grounded in playfulness, and it includes two other attributes: responsibility and reflection. Programmatically, this learning is designed into boundary-crossing intellectual activities such as learning communities and interdisciplinary seminars. We see learning defined similarly in Lee Schulman's new model for general education, which he calls a "Table of Learning" and which factors into general education attributes like reflection and engagement. What these efforts share, in addition to a capacious definition of learning, is their construction of the student as *the site for the* *yes!* *integration of a complex learning* (Booth).

   Observation Five. As Peter Elbow ("Cultures") recently noted, the teaching of literature is slowly changing, moving from a lecture-based pedagogy to one more workshop oriented, such change itself located within a larger curricular change in English studies. During the last twelve years especially, scholars have repeatedly called for a new curriculum, one sensitive to student interests, multiple expertise, and mixed media. In his afterword to the Young and Fulwiler collection *When Writing Teachers Teach Literature,* for instance, Gerald

> Faculty sometimes—perhaps too often—lament debasements in students' intellectual abilities, but our graduate programs give almost no serious or sustained attention to the pedagogical face of the problem, which therefore perpetuates itself through the educational mechanism.
> —Jerome McGann et al.

Graff suggests that "the problem [in a literature course] is to respect student experience even as we try to transform it into something different." In "Telling Our Story about Teaching Literature," Alan Purves extends Graff's point about student experience by widening the definition of literature to include various forms of presentation, including images, and creating a new purpose for such a course:

> The kinds of readers and viewers we hope to create are those who will work at the text or film and take pleasure in the intellectual *play* of working with it, and then take this experience with them and play with other texts and images, getting pleasure not simply from the experience of reading and viewing but from the thinking and talking that go with school (134–35; italics mine).

Interestingly, the aesthetics of Rosenblattian reading are linked to new forms of text and to an appreciation of the role of play in infusing and informing intellectual life.

   What these observations collectively suggest is that the academy is changing, as are the texts we consume and produce both inside and outside formal education and as is the role of literature in both education and culture at large. In response, as we shall see, several scholars and periodicals—including *College English, Teaching English in the Two-Year College, Pedagogy, ADE Bulletin,* and *Profession 2002*—have spoken to ways of changing both the teaching of literature and the education of the literature graduate students who will join the professoriate. In particular, as the recent MLA report "Professionalization in Perspective" suggests, many graduate students obtain employment at institutions where undergraduate education and general education are the stuff of pedagogical life. As important, as a companion piece by John Guillory underscores, no serious attention has been paid to pedagogical practices for the literature class, to the relationship between theory and practice, to the role of reflection in mediating between the two, or to a scholarship of teaching literature. The concerns of these scholars and institutions, of course, mirror the concerns of teachers already in the classroom who, faced with the need for innovative pedagogy, create new, theoretically informed practices that in turn can teach us much, as a quick example attests. In the *TETYC* article "Inviting Students to Challenge the American Literature Syllabus," Beverly Peterson discusses the Graffian merits of explaining the logic behind the intent of a syllabus, emphasizing its constructed nature, and inviting students to challenge the literary selections. (This is a theoretically informed pedagogy that echoes the principles of constructedness central to the material of the course.) Through such a challenge, Peterson claims, students substitute a new reading for the one originally planned by the teacher. What they choose and why and what that means for the teaching of literature— that's the scholarship of teaching.[1]

In brief, that we need to change the teaching of literature is not in question. *Why* we should change, and how—these are.

General Education and Literature: What's the Point?

Before we discuss what's *needed* for students, curriculum, or both, we might back up to consider what we aim to achieve in such a course— the literature course that participates in the general education curriculum.[2] And here we run into the first problem: although English as a discipline agrees that a general education course is valuable and important, we aren't entirely clear on what it is we want general education to accomplish, in part because what we want it to accomplish changes over time. Well over a hundred years ago, for instance, (before gen ed was invented, because *all* education was gen ed) the purpose of education was an exercise in delivery: we believed in the Arnoldian transmission of the best humanity has known and thought and said. Much of education today operates on that same belief, as Kathleen McCormick notes:

> Believing that literary texts possess timeless truths is certainly a
> dominant part of most students' literary repertoires; it is the prod-

uct of a dominant assumption of their literary educations. To assume that "great literature" is "universal" grows from a deeply ingrained ideological belief that certain cultural texts—what Matthew Arnold called "the best that has been thought and said"—contain values and experiences that are shared by most men and women in all times and places. (78)

Much like current-traditional views of writing, this view of the value of literature (and other humanities) seems to function as the default view. Directly connected to the logic of literature as the means of expressing (and sometimes problematizing) the human condition, this view of literary study is a thread that binds the changing rationales over time.

More recently, general education has been linked less to consumption of the culture and more to entering a civil and ethical discourse:

General education is, in a sense, the most amorphous part of the humanities curriculum. Its goals are perhaps less easily definable and more ambitious than the aims of a major. But the purposes that general-education courses in the humanities should serve for our students are extraordinarily important. In English courses designed for general education, students should learn to participate intelligently and ethically in the discourses of the communities to which they do and will belong as citizens. (Lloyd-Jones and Lunsford, 29)

Recent views of the role of the literature course in U.S. education sound a similar note. One seems a peculiarly American view and surprisingly utilitarian in its own way. As explained by Robert Scholes ("Transition to College Reading"), the literature course is a key to Jeffersonian democracy:

Without education, as Thomas Jefferson well understood, participatory democracy cannot function. The basis of an education for the citizens of a democracy lies in that apparently simple but actually difficult act of reading so as to grasp and evaluate the thoughts and feelings of that mysterious other person: the writer. The primary pedagogical responsibility of English teachers is to help students develop those skills. (171)

Especially in a pluralistic country, the ability to relate to the *other* is critical, and "that ability is nurtured by reading, which mediates between writer and reader" (171). More recently, scholars such as Kathleen McCormick have been interested in asking readers to engage in reading as a form of critical literacy, in which the relationship between the other and the author is examined from an ideological perspective. The outcome here involves asking students to consider how their own situatedness contributes to the way they interpret both world and text (McCormick).

Although this quick, partial account of the purposes of general education isn't intended as comprehensive, it nonetheless illustrates the shifts in education in which we participate and which we sometimes shape. As important, this brief chronology demonstrates that when it comes to general education and the literature course that is so categorized, we want it to play both intellectual and political roles in educating students.

What's the Problem?

If I ask, What's the problem?, I assume that there is in fact a problem. Readings of recent relevant publications, from MLA's *Profession* to *PMLA* to *ADE Bulletin* to *Pedagogy,* suggest that regardless of how we assess the situation—the number of students majoring in English, the number taking literature classes, the number of new faculty hires, the continuing crisis over the job market and the decline in tenure-line positions, the sense of ennui characterizing departments and the discipline at large—the delivered curriculum in literature is in some jeopardy.

Robert Scholes locates the difficulty in students' reading processes. Students read everything the same, he says. Thus, the

> The black poet, as exemplified by Gwendolyn Brooks and later Amiri Baraka, had many voices—with no voice being identified as more or less authentic. The insistence on finding one voice, one definitive style of writing and reading one's poetry, fit all too neatly with a static notion of self and identity that was pervasive in university settings.—bell hooks

problem emerges as one of difference, or otherness—a difficulty in moving from the words of the text to some set of intentions that are different from one's own, some values or presuppositions different from one's own and possibly opposed to them. This problem, as I see it, has two closely related parts. One is a failure to focus sharply on the language of the text. The other is a failure to imagine the otherness of the text's author. ("Transition to College Reading," 166)

Much like Geoffrey Sirc, Gerald Graff sees the problem as a function of our failure to link students' "street smarts" with our intellectual concerns:

> It's not a new idea, of course, that students harbor intellectual resources—"street smarts" that go untapped by formal schooling. What is not so widely noticed, however, is that these intellectual resources go unnoticed because they are tied to ostensibly

> anti-intellectual interests. We tend to assume that intellectual distinction can be manifested only with bookish subject matter—that is, that it's possible to wax intellectual about Plato, Shakespeare, the French Revolution, and nuclear fission, but not about cars, clothing fashions, dating, sports, TV, or Bible Belt religion—and we thereby overlook the intellectualism latent in supposedly philistine pursuits. ("Hidden Intellectualism," 21)

And like Scholes, Jerome McGann and his colleagues see the problem as one of reading, though they define the problem somewhat differently:

> We all know how young students, in discussing a novel, want to talk about characters (as if they were "real") and plot (as if it were a sequence of events). They usually try to "understand" characters, for example, in terms of types and in more or less generalized psychological terms. They deal with plot and events in a similarly schematic way. Events are viewed not as a structure for exposing (for example) more and more complex features of the characters, but as a sequence of connected happenings meant to interest the reader in the outcome of the fictional events (the story). In this context, we also see the students' inclination to seek thematic and conceptual interpretations of character and event, often completely abstracting away those literal textual levels that license such thematic moves. (145)

There is, McGann et al. say, a "theatricality of fiction" that students thus completely miss.

Taken together, these scholars pinpoint two sources of the "problem." Reading is a problem, and in excluding students' street smarts from the classroom, so are we.

What's the Fix?

Collectively, some of the proposed cures at least begin to paint an interesting picture of another kind of education, one much more socially constructed, more inquiry based, more informed by *reflection.*

Kathleen McCormick argues for a combined approach that brings together three schools of reading. The first approach, she says, is "a *cognitive,* information-processing model which contends that readers must actively draw on their prior knowledge to be able to process texts," an approach dominated by a pedagogy of "direct instruction"[3] (13). The second, more learner-centered approach "follows an *expressivist* model which privileges the reader and the reader's experience in the reading process" (13). The third approach, she says, is "a *social-cultural* model; it is one that privileges the cultural context in which reading occurs" (13). Partially ethnographic, partially liberation pedagogy, the hope of this approach is that it will carry out "the broader social implication of the earlier two positions." Key to McCormick's theory of reading is a dialogue among the three approaches:

> These three approaches are not diametrically opposed to each other: rather, they exist in dialectical relationship. Each acknowledges the importance of the reader, the text, and the larger social context in the reading situation, but each assigns quite different significations to the terms. While my discussion throughout privileges the social-cultural model, I am not arguing for the wholesale takeover of the other models by this model, but rather for the active development of genuine dialogue among all approaches. (14)

Robert Scholes proposes an approach we might characterize as both neoclassical and electronically wired. In thinking about the role of recitation in earlier curricula, Scholes advocates a return to a McGuffian pedagogy seemingly akin to McGann et al.'s focus on the "theatricality of fiction":

> I am not certain how close we can come to the McGuffey method in our classrooms, but I think that we should try to bridge the gap. I know that we can come very close to it in teaching drama, where the move to oral interpretation requires no explanation or apology—which is an argument for getting more drama into our courses. (" Transition to College Reading," 168)

The second change involves using electronic sources and networks to engage students:

> [N]ewer technologies also offer possibilities for the teaching of reading that we are only beginning to explore. There is a lot of writing on the Web that takes positions and makes arguments, well or badly. There are ongoing arguments, on all sorts of topics, that can be traced through particular threads on Web sites. Part of the problem we face in classrooms, especially in the general-education classrooms of colleges and in the English course of secondary schools, is that debates about literary interpretation simply do not engage many of our students. These same students, however, may go right from our classrooms to their terminals, where they engage in serious debate about issues that are important to them. (170)

Scholes specifically recommends using the Web for its "constantly replenished source of textual materials for study." Much like Graff, Scholes implicitly argues for linking our intellectual concerns with those of students, who, he says, should be invited to bring back to class "sites of interest to them" for discussion and analysis. "We need, in short," says Scholes, "to connect the development of reading and writing skills to the real world around us and to the virtual world in which that actual world becomes available to us in the form of texts" (171).

McGann et al.'s approach is located squarely in a multilayered, reiterative practice of recitation and reflection conducted in what they call "The Learner's Classroom." The faculty member, in this pedagogy, "is urged to assume a learner's posture in relation to the students and what they need to learn." Students, "in a Wittgensteinian sense," can read, they say, and beginning with what they can do is a first step.

> It is important that the students, both individually and collectively, come to see that they have these reading competencies, and also that they often don't perceive how and why they do. Coming to such realizations, students are positioned to see as well the limitations inherent in their own competencies. It is only at that point that they begin to gain access to *critical* reading skills. (147)

Just as important as the practice of critical reading is "that they [students] develop an ability to explain their judgments to others."

To carry out this pedagogy, McGann and colleagues use a reflective notebook where initial "pre-critical" moments of reading are recorded and where "a second-order process of reflection in which students could assess the relation of the two moments of reading" is also located, as is a third reflective moment. In a given unit of study, then, undergraduates

> had been moved through a triple reflective process. They had, first of all, turned reflexively on [one text, in this case] *The Bride of Lammermoor,* and on their ideas about that book, in a series of integrated classes. Second, they could see (they learned by doing) that "comparison and contrast" exercises setting two or more works in dialectical relation—in this case, Scott's and West's— could be a powerful critical tool. About the ninth week of the course, reading these novels in relation to secondary critical and theoretical works became yet another stimulus to the students' thinking. (152)

The result of this approach, according to McGann et al., is that

> students came to be able to see themselves as readers and to realize that the "meaning" of a novel is something they themselves construct on the basis of certain determinate ideas and materials; they understood that they can access the basis of their own judgments, though only with serious reflective thought. (156)

Gerald Graff's approach is more suggestive than particularized. Reflecting on his own experiences, Graff queries how "teachers can tease out the critical theory latent in student street smarts":

It certainly never dawned on me that I found the sports world more compelling than school because it was *more* intellectual than school, not less. Yet sports were full of challenging arguments, debates, problems for analysis, and meaningful statistical math in a way that school conspicuously was not. Furthermore, sports arguments, debates, and analyses made you part of a community, not just of your friends but of the national public culture. Whereas schoolwork seemingly isolated you, you could talk sports with people you had never met. Of course, schools can hardly be blamed for not making intellectual culture resemble the World Series or the Super Bowl, but schools might be learning things from the sports world about how to organize and represent intellectual culture, how to turn the intellectual game into arresting public spectacle. ("Hidden Intellectualism," 28)

A new Graffian approach would be located in both spheres, that of the academy and that of the world: "It is a matter of finding points of convergence and translation, moments when student discourse can be translated into academic discourse and vice versa, producing a kind of 'bilingualism' on both sides of the student-teacher divide" (23).

In thinking about how to reinvigorate the study of literature, then, these scholars make four principal recommendations, *all of which underscore the importance of the role that students play in their own learning:*

1. Include the drama of literature, especially through performance and oral interpretation.

2. Connect the scholarly print tradition to resources on the Web; bring the resources of one into the outcomes of the other; connect the world and its intellectual pursuits to those of the class.

3. Read and study literature individually *and* socially.

4. To misphrase E. M. Forster, "Only reflect."

We can change curriculum by design, of course. But as David Booth suggests, the best-laid plans cannot guarantee our success. Students must activate these plans, and within that dialogic relationship, learning occurs.

In "By Chance and by Design: Incidents of Learning," Booth, a professor of philosophy at St. Olaf College in Minnesota, defines what it means to learn and explains how that learning happens. To do so, he focuses on what he calls "incidents of learning, a phrase meant to point to the way learning arises out of circumstances that are only partly under the control of the people involved." A curriculum, he says,

> can be planned in minute detail; a syllabus can be planned in minute detail; a lecture can be planned at the level of each specific word. Each of these preplanned forms expresses a coordinated, synthesized, integrated arrangement of meaning in the mind of the planner. And each of these is crucial to the activity of learning. Indeed in the best of circumstances these can be the occasion of sublime inspiration. . . . [At the same time, as we know,] none of these *guarantees* that any particular curriculum, syllabus, or lecture will be the occasion of meaning making for the particular students who swing within their orbits. (n. pag.)

This observation, if accurate, raises a question: how does what Booth calls "meaning making" happen? Booth's reply is that for students, it "arises accidentally, depending on *what* they bring into the classroom, and on *how* the things they bring interact with whatever else is brought into the classroom by teachers and other students" (italics mine). In other words, all learning, depending on *teachers and other students*, is social. Just as important, learning is *situated*, depending on what students bring with them—and how they construct what they are given. As Booth argues, we can prepare for these accidents: we can

> lay down conditions for them, we can encourage one another to be on the watch for them, and to respect (even treasure) them when they occur, and we can develop ways of relating to each other that increase the chances that incidents of learning will occur. (n. pag.)

But as he suggests, the very nature of the academy—through our grading criteria and our discourse practices—tends to discourage such accidents, such serendipity. Ironically, then, by excluding the students' curricula, we can't have coherent meaning in the classroom. Or, stated as a positive,

> no matter how carefully crafted a curriculum, if coherent meanings emerge from the way elements in a curriculum are coordinated, they will emerge in *the student's own, utterly unique experience, or not at all*. Meaning is the student's achievement, and within limits that a community could probably come to agree on, the student's unique way of doing it is intrinsically worth a teacher's attention. (n. pag.)

In making his argument, Booth cites the work of various scholars, including Belenky et al.'s *Women's Ways of Knowing* and Aristotle. He focuses specifically on Aristotle's use of metaphor, claiming that Aristotle's "genius" lies in "recognizing similarity in dissimilars." It is through such recognition that coherence—and thus meaning—is made, especially between dissimilar phenomena, situated as they are in often disconnected institutional structures (such as established departments).

Here is Booth's example of such a connection: "[A] student whose literature class read Mary Shelley's *Frankenstein* might find herself thinking in an unexpected way about a unit on genetic engineering in a biology class—and vice versa." His point, of course, is that while the university

> makes no *promise* of coherence between literature and biology classes, students often discover meaningful connections of their own. And we—as individual faculty and institutions—can make a commitment to increase the *likelihood* that students will capitalize on such opportunities when they arise. (n. pag.)

Booth reminds us that our designs are always subject to chance, and he cautions us to build a curriculum that prepares and invites such fortuity.

Like Jerome McGann et al., David Booth sees in reflective practice a means of making education meaningful. In Booth's case, as in my own project, a portfolio—with its multiple reflective practices—locates the student's learning by providing texts that can chart development, allow analysis, and ground inquiry and projection.

The use of reflection to assist learning is, of course, not new.[4] John Dewey wrote extensively about reflection, most explicitly in *How We Think: A Restatement of the Relation of Reflective Thinking to the Educative Process*, where he defines reflective thinking as "the kind of thinking that consists in turning a subject over in the mind and giving it serious and consecutive consideration" (3). Reflection, he says, is goal driven; since there "is a goal to be reached, . . . this end sets a task that controls the sequence of ideas" (6). Put definitively, reflection is the "*[a]ctive, persistent, and careful consideration of any belief or supposed form of knowledge in the light of the grounds that support it and the further conclusions to which it tends*" (9). In brief, reflection is defined as goal directed and sequential, controlled by the learner because he or she wants to learn something, to solve a real problem, to resolve an ambiguous situation, or to address a dilemma (14). It relies on a dialogue between multiple perspectives as the learner contrasts the believed and the known with presuppositions and necessary conclusions.

> Our premise, which we continue to test, was that it is such reflection more than anything the teacher may say that will induce students to discover the hidden intellectual in themselves.—Gerald Graff, "Hidden Intellectualism"

Reflection, Dewey also says, is habitual and learned. "While we cannot learn or be taught to think, we do have to learn *how* to think well," he says, "especially *how* to acquire the general *habit* of reflecting" (34). Since language "connects and organizes meanings as well as selects and fixes them" (245), it follows that reflection is language specific. Dewey claims that there are three uses of language, which people develop chronologically and apply: first, the attempt to influence others; second, the entering into of intimate relations; and only later, the third, the use of language "as a conscious vehicle of thought and language" (239). The task for the educator is therefore to "direct students' oral and written speech, used primarily for practical and social ends, so that gradually it shall become a conscious tool of conveying knowledge and assisting thought" (239).

Another theorist credited with defining reflection is Lev Vygotsky. Like Dewey, he sees the exchange characteristic of interplay and dialogue as the foundation of reflection. According to Vygotsky, "Reflective consciousness comes to the child through the portals of scientific concepts" (*Thought and Language,* 171)—in other words, through the formal concepts typically learned from adults and/or in school, which are juxtaposed with "spontaneous" concepts, those unmediated by external language or systematic representation. To illustrate, Vygotsky uses the task of tying a knot:

> The activity of consciousness can take different directions; it may illuminate only a few aspects of a thought or an act. I have just tied a knot—I have done so consciously, yet I cannot explain how I did it, because my awareness was centered on the knot rather than on my own motions, the *how* of my action. When the latter becomes the object of my awareness, I shall have become fully conscious. We use *consciousness* to denote awareness of the activity of the mind—the consciousness of being conscious. (170)

Reflection, however, requires both kinds of thinking, the scientific and the spontaneous, the strength of scientific concepts deriving from their "conscious and deliberate character," the spontaneous from "the situational, empirical, and practical" (*Though and Languages,* 194). Speaking generally, Vygotsky says,

> the two processes . . . are related and constantly influence each other. They are part of a single process: the development of concept formation, which is affected by varying external and internal conditions but is essentially a unitary process, not a conflict of antagonistic, mutually exclusive forms of thinking." (157)

We see these processes in dialogue especially at certain times of development, he explains, such as when children are between the ages of seven and twelve. Then

> the child's thought bumps into the wall of its own inadequacy, and the resultant bruises—as was widely observed by J. J. Rousseau—become its best teachers. Such collisions are a powerful stimulus, evoking awareness, which in its turn, magically reveals to a child a chamber of conscious and voluntary concepts. (165)

Learning thus requires scientific concepts, spontaneous concepts, and interplay *between them.* As in the case of tying a knot, we use this dialogue to focus on the end—the knot—as well as on the processes enabling us to achieve the end.

For Vygotsky, as for Dewey, language is critical for reflection: "The relation of thought to word is not a thing but a process, a continual movement back and forth from thought to word and from word to thought." This interplay, then, is both foundational, in terms of our being human, and continuous. It begins at the moment of birth, as the child engages with—interplays with—the others of his or her environment, and according to Vygotsky , it is through this communal play and interaction that the child develops individuality:

> Piaget and others have shown that reasoning occurs in a children's group as an argument intended to prove one's own point of view before it occurs as an internal activity whose distinctive feature is that the child begins to perceive and check the basis of his thoughts. Such observations prompted Piaget to conclude that communication produces the need for checking and confirming thoughts, a process that is characteristic of adult thought. In the same way that internal speech and reflective thought arise from the interactions between the child and persons in her environment, these interactions provide the source of development of a child's voluntary behavior. (*Mind in Society*, 89–90)

In other words, we learn to understand ourselves through explaining ourselves to others. To do this, we rely on a reflection that involves a *checking* against, a *confirming*, and a *balancing* of self with others (12–13).

More recently, philosopher Donald Schön ("Causality") has offered another, related theoretical perspective from which to view both teaching and learning, the perspective that frames much of my work in this project. Known principally for his definition of the reflective practitioner, Schön argues that it is by reflecting on our own work—by knowing it, by reviewing it, by discerning patterns in it, by projecting appropriately from those patterns, and by using such projections to hypothesize a new way of thinking about a situation—that we theorize our own practices and that we come to know and understand our work and perhaps thus to improve it. In other words, reflection is *rhetorical.*

In explaining the connection of reflection to epistemology, Schön ("Causality") begins by distinguishing between two kinds of knowing: that of the technical realm and that of the nontechnical. The world of technical rationality, Schön says, allows for a knowing by way of causal inference that is controlled: the lab experiment, for instance, that confirms the presence of an antibody in the blood. This world is neat, clean, controlled, and therefore managed quite neatly.

The second world is the world in which we *live*—and it is certainly the world of the classroom—the world where causal inference is a judgment call, no matter how well informed. Such knowledge relies on the expertise of its participants who, through reflection-in-action—a rethinking "lead[ing] to on-the-spot experiment and further thinking that affects what we do" (Schön, "Causality" 29)—become skillful improvisers. Given that students work in this second world—the world of teaching and learning—they must find effective ways to ground and to exercise both inquiry and judgment. Equally important, Schön says, it is only through reflection that they—and we—are better able to accommodate ourselves to the next iteration of a similar instance:

> In normal social science, the choice of questions, the selection of variables, and the design of experiments are all designed to produce externally valid causal generalizations of the covering law type. In contrast, causal inquiry in organizations typically centers on a particular situation in a single organization, and when it is successful, it yields not covering laws but prototypical models of causal pattern that may guide inquiry in other organizational situations—prototypes that depend, for their validity, on modification and testing "in the next situation." "Reflective transfer" seems to me a good label for this kind of generalization." (97)

Key to Schön's perspective, then, are two kinds of reflection. Reflection-in-action is the process of thinking about the nature of a practice while that practice is ongoing. Reflective transfer is the process of thinking that allows us to generalize from specifics, to develop schemata and other models that move us from one specific instance to another, and to create a prototype that lends itself to transfer (50–51). In other words, through reflective transfer we create the specific practice from which we may derive principles toward *prototypical models.* Not least, the ability to *see oneself so generalize* contributes to identity formation.

Through reflection and awareness, a reader is developed.

What follows in subsequent chapters is one attempt to think about what it might mean as a curricular matter to make the student the site for learning literature in a general education literature class. I focus on the gen ed class as a prototype, although it can take several forms. The effort, generally, is to help students:

1. Read
2. Read critically and appreciatively
3. Read reflectively
4. Connect these readings to the world and back
5. Understand the differences between kinds of readings and texts
6. Make associations and create habits of mind that will influence their practices and judgments as they go forward

Much of our thinking about literature has focused elsewhere, perhaps rightly so, on the college student planning to teach middle or secondary school, for example, and on the English major. But as we see in the proposals of McCormick and Scholes and Graff and McGann et al., we are still in search of what we want the general education literature class to do.[5] Equally important, as I think about such a course and as I construct this curriculum, I also want to think about how reflection needs to be woven into the curriculum.

> The work of general education is critical inquiry and critical exchange. The fundamental commitment underlying this work is the giving of reasons. When high school teachers ask me, as they often do, what they should teach their students, this is what I answer. Don't teach them writing. Don't teach them reading. Teach them the habit of giving reasons for what they think, and explain how reading and writing can help them do this.—James Slevin

I'll begin by thinking about the curriculum that students bring in the door with them: *the lived curriculum*. As Anne Gere has shown, students learn well in sites other than schools.[6] And even when they are school learners, no student walks in the door as a blank slate. Each one brings with him or her a set of prior courses and experiences and connections that contextualize the delivered curriculum. How, we might ask, can we tap that lived curriculum when students enter the course, invite it into the course not only as a way to engage students but also as intellectual activity in its own right, and, not least, as a means of linking to the delivered curriculum? Just as important, if we want students to carry the course forward in a living way, we might think about making that future connection part of the curriculum.

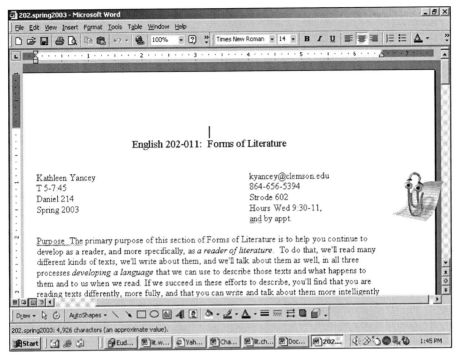

Figure 1.1

A second curriculum, the one we are most familiar with, is the *delivered curriculum,* the one we design. We see it in syllabi, where course goals are articulated (see Figure 1.1). We see it in assignments, where students deal with the specifics of the curriculum. We see it in readings, where students enter a specific discourse and specific ways of thinking. We see it in the vocabulary of the course. Given that the students in a general education literature course are not novices in the discipline, but rather potential members of a reading public, we see it in our desire that students continue to engage with the processes and materials of the course once it has concluded.

The third curriculum is the *experienced curriculum.* I observed earlier that my family and I go to the same film but see different movies; we both share that experience and don't. Likewise, students come to the same course, but that course differs somewhat from one person to the next (Yancey, "Teacher Portfolios"). Inviting that experienced curriculum into the course, making it visible and thus accessible and indeed legitimate, is yet another task we might assign ourselves.

The next three chapters—"The Lived Curriculum," "The Delivered Curriculum," and "The Experienced Curriculum: Closing the

> But reading is interactive: all readers concretize the meanings of the texts within the frameworks provided by their own repertoires. They bring their own associations to help make meanings from texts, and their readings may therefore often be quite different from the writer's or the original audience's. Readers will understand and interpret texts differently not just because of their psychological profiles or personality types, however, as reader-response critics would have it, but rather for culturally specific reasons—because they bring different gender-specific, race-specific, generation-specific or culture-specific questions to their reading.—Kathleen McCormick

Circle"—speak to these curricula, showing the logic of each, illustrating the logic through assignments and student responses, and exploring in the process how reflective practice is a necessary corollary of literature practice. In Chapter 5, we review a culminating activity, the literature portfolio, by exploring two genres of such portfolios, the print and the digital, showing how to move from one to the next, and arguing that the virtues of one are quite different from the virtues of the other. Not least, in Chapter 6 we conclude by thinking about how all this fits together and what it means for a new literature practice, and by considering the kind of questions prompted by this approach as well as some future explorations worth considering.

The postsecondary institution of learning is organized into boxes—departments and programs and centers and colleges. If there is to be integration, the student will be its locus. If we understand where that site of integration is—within multiple curricula—and if we provide space for all three such curricula as well as dialogue between them, we may find that our students learn more as well as other than we anticipate.

Notes

1. It's also fair to note that students exercise choice as a substitute only when they "win" a challenge.

2. General education is hardly a unified construct, as we know. Portland State University, for example, bundles it all into a set of vertical, team-taught interdisciplinary seminars, and to good effect; many places use cafeteria models, in which students often choose from a buffet of courses, sometimes on the basis of time the course is taught (rather than as a construction of an intellec-

tual or academic plan for development); other schools are moving to a more outcomes-based model.

3. As Anne Gere and her colleagues show, the cognitive model doesn't have to presume direct instruction: see Ellis, Gere, and Lamberton.

4. The following discussion is adapted from *Reflection in the Writing Classroom* by Kathleen Blake Yancey. Reprinted by permission of Utah State University Press.

5. Ironically, we have of course thought about the general education literature class as part of the *writing* curriculum, as the work of Young and Fulwiler, for instance, attests. But most of us haven't thought very hard or well about what such a course ought to do outside of that context.

6. The term *lived curriculum* is in some ways similar to Gere's use of *extracurriculum*. As she notes,

> Arthur Applebee also uses the term "extracurricular," but for him it describes one of three traditions—the ethical, the classical, and the extracurriculum—from which English studies emerged. Applebee defines the extracurriculum as the nonacademic tradition that contributed to the development of English studies. Like Rudolph, he employs their term extracurriculum to describe eighteenth and nineteenth century college literary clubs and recounts how these groups discussed vernacular literature not judged worthy of academic study. As Applebee explains, college literary clubs also sponsored libraries, speakers, and magazines, providing a context where students could "polish their skills in English composition" (12). Applebee's extracurriculum does not include fraternities or athletic groups, but it confirms Rudolph's point that the extracurriculum lent undergraduates power in American colleges because the curriculum was adapted to their interests. Gerald Graff emulates Applebee's description of extracurricular literary clubs, noting their contribution to the development of English studies. (79)

Gere also notes this usage of *extracurriculum* to describe "a white male enterprise" (79) that "positions the extracurriculum as a way-station on the route toward a fully professionalized academic department, thereby implying that the extracurriculum withered" once its work was done. My use of the term *lived curriculum* thus borrows some of the same experience in that it acknowledges the curriculum occurring outside of institutional educational sites. At the same time, it includes all learning prior to the site in question.

2 The Lived Curriculum

I believe content is a part of process, which is essential to technique and form.

Yusef Komunyakaa

As I was once reminded—"I was by no means aliterate when school started this semester"—students do not enter our classes as blank slates. Before entering college, most students have completed twelve years of official, formal study of literature. This *delivered curriculum* has included picture books and narratives in elementary school; adventure stories, adolescent literature, and canonical literature in middle school; and more canonical literature in high school (Applebee). In all three settings, many teachers, as we see in the work of teacher scholars such as Lucy Calkins, Nancie Atwell, and Carol Jago, go beyond the canonical, including as well both noncanonical literature and student-*selected* literature. Others, like Tom Romano and Wendy Bishop, approach literature by treating nonfiction and fiction side by side, often with student-*created* literature. At the same time, in high school particularly, the study of literature is influenced by external factors, among them state testing programs and test-based curricula such as the Advanced Placement and the International Baccalaureate programs. Especially in the era of No Child Left Behind, known in many teaching circles as No Child Left Untested, testing has new salience for teachers and students alike.

> In the past I would read, at least for classes, like I would be tested on every little item in the book, and that really took a lot of the enjoyment out of the reading experience. And that is pretty much how I started the semester, reading to try and find the "universal" theme and trying to remember each insignificant detail because this was an English class and that is how you learn about literature; there is always a right interpretation, and right way to read a novel, poem, play, etc.—David

Unfortunately, the prominence given these tests—by the culture at large as well as by parents and school districts—can in effect rewrite any literature curriculum. Or, given the ubiquity of literature testing, it's easy to see why students might think of the literature curriculum aliteratively, as not-quite-totally texts for tests.[1]

It's also the case that many high school teachers look to what is expected in college literature classes as a way to think about literary study for their own classes. In part, teachers want to align their curricula with college curricula so as to prepare their students going on to college. Current statistics suggest that over 50 percent of high school gradu-ates continue their education in some postsecondary school, and pre-paring these students well is one outcome that high school teachers of-ten seek. In part, teachers want to see what questions college faculty are pursuing in order to keep their own teaching current; we see this impulse working institutionally through NEH literature seminars and graduate curricula. What high school teachers will discover in the col-lege setting *is* quite interesting if they look at courses designed for the English major: provocative courses connected to digital technology, as at the University of California, Santa Barbara program in digital cultures, and cultural studies courses that have all but swept higher education generally, to cite but two examples. Curiously, however, when they look at the sophomore literature course for the non-English major—and non-English majors make up something in excess of 90 percent of college students—they'll find a mix almost without pattern. Some courses, for instance, are surveys of British and American literature, intended prin-cipally for the English major, not for the gen ed student; these courses are remarkably similar to the literature curricula students found in high school. Some courses focus on special topics linked to pop culture and/ or film, like the gen ed lit course at UNC Charlotte in children's litera-ture that includes each text in its print form as well as in its film form, with a heavy emphasis on Disney. Still other courses are stand-alones that seem to fit with the mission of the department—courses in Native American literature when that is an area of emphasis for the department, or Southern literature that represents the hosting region of the school and a special area for the department. The *delivered* curriculum of lit-erature for purposes of general education, in other words, seems, on the one hand, remarkably similar to the delivered curriculum students have engaged in for their first twelve years of schooling. On the other hand, when the courses are different, they seem designed to accommodate the needs of faculty or to highlight departmental strengths, worthy pur-poses in their own way. More generally, however, it's not clear what outcomes or ends this delivered curriculum writ large—which has a twofold special purpose: first, as the end of the cumulative literature curriculum, and second, as fitting within general education—is intended to serve.

In addition to this delivered curriculum, students have spent a lifetime engaged in their own *lived curriculum. Many*, though not all, learned about reading experientially on a parent's or grandparent's knee. Such reading is infused with affect, the sensation of sharing some-thing wonderful, both textually and interpersonally. This reading, of course, often contrasts with the reading done in school, in part because someone else—at the school or state or district level—chooses the texts; in part because as students progress, reading shifts from social to isolated and independent activity; in part because the reading often culminates in a test, which provides an inescapable context that changes the reading game. *Many students,* though not all, have used reading instrumentally, to learn—about sex, video games, or computer documentation, etc.—in many different kinds of texts: magazines and books; short stories and Web pages; user manuals; game protocols and player identifications; and, not least, literature itself, though too often in texts that are banned from schools. In Rosenblatt's terms, this reading can be both efferent and aesthetic: concurrently purposeful and engaging, utilitarian and pleasing and artful. For some students, this reading too contrasts with in-school reading, which seems not purposeful, often mysterious, and needlessly cryptic. *Many students,* though not all, read for fun, although not necessarily the texts we recommend: Booker Prize winners are left on the shelf in favor of Stephen King. Others write their own literature; some perform this literature—or that written by someone else—and too often what is performed does not meet our standards for literature.[2]

> Further, in school, particularly in English class, we often act as though reading involves only one kind of legitimate printed matter—all else does not qualify. In this way, we jettison much nonfiction and almost all technical works; we scorn the contemporary and even the pop as if they are not real reading, certainly not worthy of our time. Inadvertently, or sometimes directly, we tell our students that reading is only Keats or Austen or Morrison, never *Sports Illustrated* or Stephen King or *Chicken Soup for the Teenage Soul.* We thus tell students that the reading world is a very small one with fairly rigid boundaries. This is not encouraging or inviting, and many of our students accordingly decline to enter that little, circumscribed country of what we narrowly define as reading.—Leila Christenbury

In sum, when students walk into the general education literature class, they know quite a bit about both reading and literature, some of it from formal schooling, some of it from what Anne Gere calls the extracurriculum—together an amalgamation of formal and informal experience that students bring with them into our classrooms and that is here called the lived curriculum.

‰

One way to begin mapping the lived curriculum is to explore a set of three explicit questions that function as a heuristic. Through these questions, students are prompted first to think in terms of specific reading practices, and second, on the basis of that thinking, to reflect on them and make meaning.

Name something you have liked reading, and explain why. This question begins where students are, with a reading that students like. Such a reading seems foundational in a literature class, which from one perspective *is* a class in reading. If I knew what students liked to read, I reasoned, perhaps I could link to or build on those texts or on the kinds of texts they cited. Alternatively, students might cite texts we could use for contrast—the magazine *Maxim* is no poem—and, as the Summerfields have demonstrated, contrast provides a powerful frame for thinking. Also, if I asked this question formally, I would be inviting students to self-identify as people who do engage in the central required activity of the course: reading. From a Burkean perspective, then, this invited identity could provide a segue into the course: students reading are literature students in the making.

Name something you dislike reading, and explain why. Following the logic of *Embracing Contraries* (Elbow), students are asked to identify a text they don't like. It's fair (enough) for people to like some readings and to dislike others. In fact, such likes and dislikes can provide the beginnings of an interesting discussion. (As someone who wrote a thesis on Theodore Dreiser, I never tire of explaining why I like his work and why I think it's "good," but I also understand that this is a lonely position. Likewise, there are texts I dislike—John Updike's work comes to mind—and I've had wonderful arguments about the value of those texts.) I also thought that if I asked students why they disliked a particular text, we could see if there were patterns across the answers (there are) and use those as a way of contextualizing our own work.

Based on these evaluations, who are you as a reader? This cumulative question asks students to review the practices they have just recorded and to draw some conclusions based on this prior thinking. As we know from Donald Schön (*Educating*), reflection often works from the specifics to the general. Here students are asked to record practice, analyze it, and then generalize from those observations. What would students say about themselves as readers, I wondered, if those observations were located in the particulars of specific texts, especially if I made it clear that all texts—from e-mail to newspapers, from novels to drama— "counted" as texts. And what might I learn from their answers?

So I asked.

One piece of material that I really like to read is USA Today. The reason for this is because I like to know what is going on around the world. I enjoy reading quick things that let me know what is going on right away. There are hundreds of newspapers, but the USA Today includes a wide variety of topics that interest me. Not only does it focus on the news, but it includes entertainment, business, and many other things. I also like it because newspapers are very easy for me to read. Newspaper articles get my attention really quick and keep it the whole time that I am reading.

Something I do not like to read are long novels. The reason for this is because while trying to read them I kind of zone out. Even with novels that have a theme that I like I still get lost in them. Also, I am kind of an impatient person and when I start reading something I want to get finished pretty quick. I am also not a very fast reader and I get frustrated sometimes when reading a long book because I feel like I am never going to finish it.

As a reader I believe that reading for me is something that I do not really enjoy to some extent. I need to be drawn into the reading very quickly and my attention needs to be held all throughout. One thing I do like to do when reading is visualizing it. I get more entertained by what I am reading when I do this. When I sit down to read something I want to be able to finish it right there. I do realize though that this is something that cannot be done all of the time and I must learn to correct it.

—Cade

Cade's reflection is fairly common, both in its choices and in its values. Like Cade, students do read; the good news here is that he reads often and that reading seems to be a habit. At the same time, his principal values for reading are *quick* and *easy,* and the principal text is a short and highly visual one given more to description than analysis, values that are, of course, somewhat at odds with the values of literature.[3] There is motivation behind these values: Cade says that when a text is short and visual, maintaining attention isn't a problem. Of course, if he can't maintain enough attention to read the text, we won't be able to work with it in class. And the *quickness* serves another purpose: "I need to be drawn into the reading very quickly and my attention needs to be held all throughout." Much like an unpracticed writer, this reader needs to move into the text quickly and needs it to end fast as well; otherwise, frustration sets in and he is likely to "zone out." Cade isn't totally at the mercy of the text, however: he says he likes to visualize texts and that he understands he needs to learn to sustain his own reading, to "correct," as he says, the way he now tries to finish (too) quickly. The role of school for a reader like Cade is crucial. Through a delivered curriculum that includes reading practice generally, Cade might learn to read rhetorically, for a specific purpose, according to the conventions of a genre. Likewise, Cade might learn strategies beyond the visual that can help him sustain reading behavior. More generally, Cade needs to find his own ways to read, as well as his own reasons. And these goals are a function of the lived curriculum he brings into the class with him.

Other students make other observations that, again, can help the class begin to create a foundation for thinking about different kinds of reading. For instance, a surprising number of students claim that they like the readings in their courses:

> I know myself as a reader. I am not interested in stories or long novels. This is just my preference. I read what I am assigned in school, but for enjoyment I read magazines, WebPages, emails, and material that offers me knowledge that I actually care to obtain and use in the future. For instance, I enjoy learning about my body or future careers. I don't consider myself a feminist, but I truly enjoyed learning all of the material involved with women's studies.
>
> —Emily

Like Cade, Emily doesn't like long novels or even stories, and given the nature of the course—which is dominated by novels and stories—this isn't good news. At the same time, Emily is thinking on the page, in this reflection learning about herself as a reader. Although she begins by claiming a preference for nonschool texts—"WebPages, emails, and material that offers me knowledge that I actually care to obtain and use"—she follows the associations where they take her, in this case to "the material involved with women's studies." Put differently, while she maintains her stance as an efferent reader, she finds that her reading preferences aren't as dichotomous—nonschool texts are useful, school texts are not—as she had thought. Writing the reflection has helped Emily see who she perceives herself to be as a reader, and it's not quite the reader-self she claimed at the start.

In still other cases, aware that the identity they bring in the door doesn't match the preferred identity of the class, students write a reflection indicating a willingness to develop the new identity:

> I would first like to let you know that I am not a very enthusiastic reader. Reading is not something that comes "naturally" to me. I cannot read very quickly, and it is difficult for me to visualize what is going on in the story. I would much rather take the "work" out of it by watching the movie. Lately, though, I've had an interest in becoming a better reader, so if you can help me to enjoy the

process, I am very willing to make the effort it may require. Well, I just wanted to provide you with a little insight into my situation. Thanks for the time.

—Carrie

A moviegoer, this student also cannot visualize and cannot read quickly: in the era of the microwave, speed is a virtue, and reading doesn't seem to offer that. At the same time, however, this student is willing, she says, to "make the effort" to become a "better reader." She'd also like to "enjoy the [reading] process." Based on Carrie's lived curriculum, we have another place to begin.

Not least are those students who *like* to read:

We all have "reading personalities" and in this essay I will be examining myself as a reader. . . . I'm the type of reader who puts myself into the novel, in other words I pretend to be the main character(s). It gives me a sense of freedom to be able to pick up a book and be transferred to another place and time. This is one of the good things about books when compared to movies. When watching a movie you're doing just that, watching. While reading a book on the other hand one has to use their imagination more and create the world the book is describing, leaving the story open to interpretation and therefore making it "yours."

—Harriet

Given the influence of peers on peers, if I can get Harriet talking to Carrie, they may both become better, smarter readers.

A common way to bring the lived curriculum into class is to invite students to bring what they know, especially about key ideas, to the (reading) table. For instance, in beginning Frank Norris's novel *The Octopus,* I often ask students to share what they know about related contexts and concepts; we use that collective knowledge as a way of introducing multiple stories inside a novel. I also learn a great deal about the students, such as the fact that increasingly they see Westerns as television shows that their parents watch; epics as what the movies show; and novels as having

> Western
> Westerns involve the wild west and cowboys. I see people like Festus and Matt Dillion in "Gunsmoke," the television show, when I think about the western genre. Horses and a cattle drive, barbecue sauce and other things of the sort come to mind also. It involves sheriffs and outlaws; gunfights and standoffs are also included.—Reggie

three elements—plot, theme, and narrator. And where the students are wrong—all epics are poems, so I've also been told—we can talk, but only because we asked.

> I'm invisible in this class every day.

> I seriously believe that people with mental and physical disabilities are very much invisible in the world. My mother and all of her sisters and all of my father's sisters work for different disability boards in the Low Country and I cannot list the thousands of times that they have talked about how the rights of those who are unable to do for themselves are over-looked. During the summer I am a camp counselor for children and teens with disabilities and when we take them places, business owners would rather hide the individuals with disabilities in corners or private rooms because they are different. My Uncle has a mental disability and he has told my mother and myself of numerous occasions when people have overlooked him because of it. This invisibil-ity is very bad.—Sammie

Other times students are asked to connect their lived curriculum to the theme of the delivered curriculum. Often

> The most meaningful reading I have done this year would have to be the novel *Invisible Man*. Since invisibility [is] reflected onto culture and society, it is something . . . which I can apply to the real world. Now I try not to look past the homeless, poverty-stricken, disabled, less-advantage, and elder people. I know that in my own experiences, I did not like the feeling of being invisible, so I can assume that others do not [either]. I learned that even though America dwells on equality, there really is not such a thing. Perhaps someday, everyone will be treated equally but it is going to be a long time in order for everyone to get past the stereotypes. *The Invisible Man* taught me a lot about society and the multiple meanings of invisibility. Even the group presentations reflected how significant invisibility is in our culture.
> —Ryan

I link two novels—*Invisible Man,* for ex-ample, and *The House of Mirth*—that in many ways are unlike each other, but that share a concern for a narrator who becomes increasingly invisible. To begin such a unit, I pose four tasks:

1. Define invisibility.
2. Identify a time when you were invisible, and describe it.
3. Was this invisibility a good thing or a bad thing?
4. Who is invisible in our culture, and is this good or bad?

Students begin with simple definitions, which they revisit as the term progresses. They all have experienced invisibility, sometimes in relief when they didn't want to be noticed, other times in moments of pain (the occasion of divorcing parents is mentioned frequently), still other times in moments of ambivalence. And they see that while invisibility can on occasion be good, it's probably not so good in the long term. The culture, they say, is filled with invisible people, from the disabled to the aged, from the Down syndrome child to the Clemson bus driver and the Clemson janitorial staff—and none of these, they say, is a "good" invisibility. At the same time, persons from the Middle East are now more visible than before in the United States, and this, they say, is a "bad" visibility.

These questions about the lived curriculum, asked individually, are shared collectively; they set the stage for the delivered curriculum.

Another way to think about the lived curriculum invites students to make a connection between the object of study, in this case literature, and the culture at large. Sometimes, of course, we make those connections for students; it's common in a successful math class (i.e., one that succeeds for students) for the faculty member to show how the abstractions of a formula can help solve particular problems in the culture. Likewise, teachers make connections as a means of comparison and contextualization: explaining the class system as depicted in a Victorian novel and comparing it with today's class system, in both the United Kingdom and in the United States, can help students appreciate the frustration that Jude (the Obscure) experiences in Hardy's eponymous novel. Asking *students* to make such connections—not to contextualize a specific work, but rather to engage in an informal, playful thought experiment—might, I thought, be engaging and creative, a way of inviting the recognition of "similarities in dissimilars" that David Booth advocates. The key, of course, is that the person making the connections is the student.

> Do you see poetry in the culture? Where? And how is what you see poetic?

> I think that poetry is found in more things than just movies. I love to listen to classical music. To me, this is a from [sic] of poetry. Just as a poem uses words and patterns to create feelings in a poem, music uses musical notes, patterns, and words to induce feelings.

The comparison between poetry and music seems exactly the kind we might make in school, and it shows students that they know more than they think they do, that they should articulate their intuitions, and that often they should trust them. Sometimes that intuitive knowing has been schooled; other times this is less true. Both kinds belong in the classroom.

Other comparisons are more unexpected, at least to me:

> The other day I was watching the football game and I noticed that the whole game is a poem. You can't look at one line of poetry and make sense of it[,] the same way that you can't look at one play and make total sense of the overall plan. Each line in a poem leads to the next the same way that each football play sets up the next.

With the students' permission, I bring such connections into class, sometimes as a set of student observations that shows the kinds and range of associations, sometimes as just a single association. Using a comparison like this one as an introduction to the reading of a poem allows me to read a poem with the class, working back and forth from the poem to the description—"Each line in a poem leads to the next the same way that each football play sets up the next"—creating an association that (I hope) will now contextualize the reading of poetry more generally for the class.

Some observations are more sustained:

> An example of poetry in the culture in today's world is a large city where there are many pedestrians walking around going to different places for different reasons at different speeds. This is a very diverse group of people doing many different things. Businessmen and women walk briskly from tall building to building in their suits and holding their briefcases. City workers such as police officers, firemen, and garbage collectors hurry about doing their jobs. Students hurry back and forth from class to class with their books in hand. People deliver packages to places and mailmen going around collecting the day's mail. Look around and you will see young teenagers with nothing to do but play around just trying to kill time. Old people slowly amble along admiring the scenery while a new mother rides her baby around in his stroller. It is poetic to me how all these different people move around going different places unknown to each other, but move with each other in harmony.
>
> —Cade

Like the initial explicit reflective questions, these observations are (other) starting places. Later in the term, we'll consider whether a novel is poetic, and if so, how; if a drama is novelistic, and again, if so, how. Students know more about literature than they think, and when asked, they can be creative in discerning the poetic in life as well as in text.

An image created by Gertrude Stein (see Figure 2.1) always makes me wonder, Is this poetry? Often I bring the image into class and ask the same question. The class divides rather neatly into three parties: a precious few who think it's a poem, those in the majority who are certain it is not, and the uncertains. Typically, by the end of the discussion, the distribution of sentiment has changed, as have the language and the questions. The question "Is it a poem?" invites a definition of poetry and soon morphs into the related questions "Is it poetic?" and "If so, how?" I'm not, as you may imagine, interested in a right or wrong answer, and that is the point: it's about the reasoning, about the feeling, about the thinking.

Figure 2.1

During one semester, while visiting the campus of University of California, Davis, I walked into what I would call a sculpture garden, a space called "Stone Poem" (see Figure 2.2). I found myself engaging in the same assignment I had given the students earlier.[4] Admittedly, the title of the garden, in announcing the sculpture as poem, gave me the answer, but I wasn't so sure. I brought this query, a real one for me as well as for the students, into class. Was this a poem? (Presumably the artist believed so.) Was it even poetic? It was intentional, yes. It had form. It was suggestive. Was there a discourse community that would construct the same interpretation, a similar meaning from experiencing it?

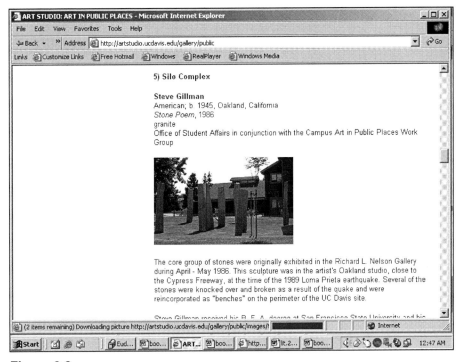

Figure 2.2

Was it imagistic? Symbolic? Was the form in fact the content? (Was it, then, like e. e. cummings's "r-p-o-p-h-e-s-s-a-g-r"?)

Such thought experiments—and they can be prompted by any number of events and places around us—help us all make connections between literature and the culture because they require us to think through what we believe poetry is and why. This kind of exercise isn't, of course, only an exercise. When practiced in the context of a delivered literature curriculum, it can lead to insights about poetry and about what makes it good, as one student explains:

> Before this course, I knew what a poem was, yet never really had thought about what made a poem. During the term we were frequently asked if certain poems were good poems or not. We were to respond with an answer and a reason why we thought it was either/or. This was especially helpful because this stimulated me to think about what makes a good poem and identify these elements in each poem. By doing this, I came to my working definition of what makes a poem (something I did not have before). The development of our thoughts on poetry was not strictly confined to the realm of written poetry. We were also confronted

with images of poems that were atypical [such as a sculpture garden called] "stone poem" and the new design for the World Trade Center. Within these exercises we were to tell whether the image was a poem or not and, depending on the answer, what the elements were that made it poetic. This was especially challenging. This exercise was very effective because I had never before considered that an image, a sculpture, a design, etc. could be a poem. However, now I know that there can indeed be other manifestations of a poem. Even more, I learned that there is not often a right or wrong answer to the question of whether or not an image, sculpture, design is poetic. If the answer that is given is thoughtful and supported with evidence and a working definition of the factors that compose a poem, the answer cannot usually be disregarded as wrong.

—Will

In 2002, I met a student in first-year comp whose skill in graphic communication allowed her to map her writing process. When I saw Ashley's map—which uncannily resembles the "maps" produced in the Flower and Hayes research on writing process—I thought how helpful such mapping might be when applied to reading (see Figures 2.3 and 2.4).

When students enter our classrooms, they also bring with them reading processes that are largely unarticulated. Asking students to map these processes might help them articulate the processes. I also knew that such a request would be tricky. Although both writing and reading are practices that in some ways are abstract, the writing process leaves material traces of itself—notes and drafts and comments on drafts. These are useful in constructing a map, as are the processes (such as peer review) staged in class. By contrast, reading, at least in my classes, too often doesn't seem to have a process, not even a trace of one. Students trained well by public schools to return books unblemished or pay a fine enter a college culture in which selling their books back is the bookend to buying them. The books with the highest resale value are clean books. Equally important, even if students do take notes, highlight, and indeed write on texts, reading still seems an abstraction. As Robert Scholes ("Transition") has noted, you can't see it. You can't hear it. All evidence of how we read, then, is secondhand at best. And then, too, mapping how we read could distort the reading process, I knew. I still thought that it was worth trying.

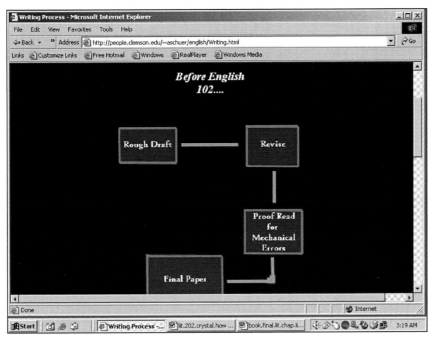

Figure 2.3

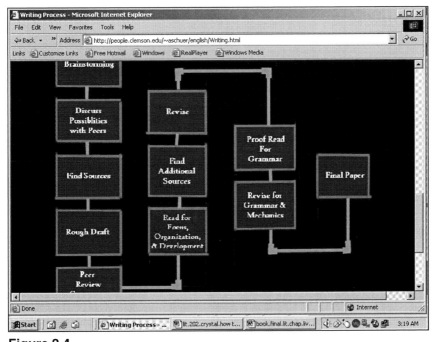

Figure 2.4

I invited students to map a poem they had read. Choose only one poem, I said, and map your reading process. At the end of the term, I invited students to re-map reading a poem. Sammie's maps are illustrative (see Figures 2.5 and 2.6). Like Ashley, over the term she developed an elaborated process. Just as interesting is what changes from one map to the next. In the first map (Figure 2.5), the strategies Sammie deploys are limited and redundant. Of the nine "moves," half of them are located not in moving but in *stopping:* "confusion," "confusion," "read up to the confusing part," "get frustrated," and "stop." What seems plotted here, then, is the analogue to writer's block: *reader's block.*

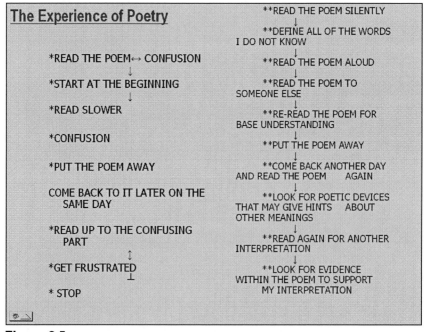

Figure 2.5

By the end of the term, Sammie has both discarded processes and acquired others, and reader's block seems to have been resolved into several productive strategies (see Figure 2.6). Confusion, rather than appearing as an obstacle, now motivates several actions, among them "defin[ing] all of the words" she doesn't know, "read[ing] the poem aloud" and "to someone else," "read[ing] again for another interpretation," and "look[ing] for evidence within the poem." The map by itself, of course, is a single representation; it does not substitute for a reading of a poem. But as a mechanism for showing students how they read, it's helpful. Moreover, when students compare their maps with those of others, they find in the comparison a means of analysis and a number of other strategies. Not least, when such a map tells the same story that we see in more formal assignments—a close reading of a poem matching an "elaborated" reading map—we can speak with greater confidence about how well a student is progressing.

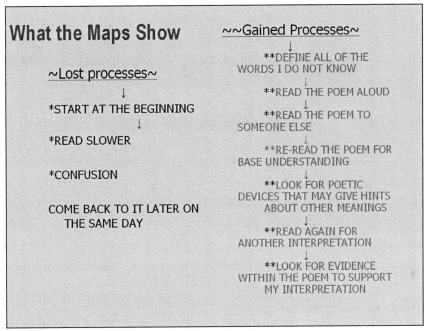

Figure 2.6

Crystal's experience is similar to Sammie's, although she speaks of the ways she now thinks about reading different kinds of texts (see Figure 2.7); her story shows us another value of such mapping.

> This class has not been the only class that I was required to read. As with this class, textbooks are required for my other courses. Textbooks are a bit difficult for me to read. I think that this class has taught me that different types of literature require a person to read a certain way. I would not read a novel the same way that I would read a textbook. When reading an interesting novel, I'm able to read for hours, or even until the book is finished. Before this class, I would try to read chapters at a time from a textbook. I have realized that I must read textbooks in sections. If I can't read a chapter at a time, then I should read certain sections at a time.

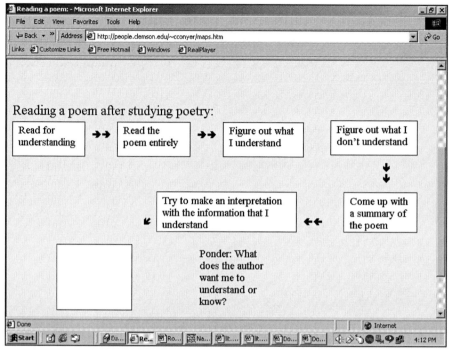

Reading a poem after studying poetry:

| Read for understanding | → → | Read the poem entirely | → → | Figure out what I understand | | Figure out what I don't understand |

Try to make an interpretation with the information that I understand

Come up with a summary of the poem

Ponder: What does the author want me to understand or know?

Figure 2.7

Also, I find myself reading aloud more when reading textbooks. I do this because I believe that I'm able to retain the information more when reading aloud. Also, I need to be in a strictly non-distracting area to read textbooks. I can be easily distracted when reading textbooks more than if I was reading a novel.

Mapping, then, provides students with another means of understanding their own work, of bringing into the class their lived curriculum and using it as a way of planning for difference.

Most students will complete the course. If they have satisfied the general education literature requirement, they are likely to have completed as well the *entire* delivered literature curriculum of a lifetime. That's not a consoling thought, I have to concede. The course, it seems to me (and there is some evidence to support this perception), does a good job of helping students continue as voluntary readers, begin to read in a more sophisticated way, and make connections to the culture at large. But of course it doesn't do enough. If this is their last literature course, and if

I want these students to join the informed reading public, what else might I do? How could I connect with the lived curriculum that will be these students' entire literature curriculum on completion of the course? The following assignment was one effort to do just that, create such a connection:

> The Assignment: You do have one assignment for next week, and it connects nicely with break, which in theory is a time when you might read for leisure. :) Given this as a context, you will review a book—either fiction or non-fiction—based on the first chapter of that book. First chapters of the books you may choose from are available on the web for the *New York Times*. Please review this book for the members of the class and recommend that they read it, or not.

Students read all kinds of chapters, some fiction, some nonfiction. They reported to the class:

> The first few lines in *A Ship Made of Paper,* by Scott Spencer captured my attention because two characters in the book were introduced as having conflict with each other. As I continued to read the excerpt, I enjoyed Spencer's style of writing. The many descriptive words used helped me understand the setting and become comfortable with the novel. I like the comparison Spencer made in relating a ten minute drive with a four year-old to there being "something tender at the center of creation, some meaning, some purpose and poetry" in life. I would recommend this book to others because from this excerpt there seems to be some eventful things that will take place. The book does not seem to be boring. This excerpt has sparked my interest to the point, I will definitely read it.
>
> —Janeen

And some of them did. Equally important, they now have a source and a strategy should they decide they want to read, want to see what's being published and what's available. What Janeen said as the class concluded makes this point. Time is precious, she says, and while she wants to read, she wants a bit of a preview. This assignment showed her how books could be previewed. And it's *free*. Much like seeing a preview in a theater or hearing a cut from a CD on the radio, the *New York Times* Web site can show students a cut from the book that might lead to them reading the entire volume.

The lived curriculum represents a set of rich experiences; tapping that curriculum means inviting it into the classroom in a number of different ways. Finally, it's the *mix* of invitations that encourages a readiness to learn, as Harriet explains:

> At the beginning of the semester, Dr. Yancey asked everyone in the class to think about the way in which we go about reading a piece of literature and develop a map that illustrates that process. This seemed like an odd and irrelevant assignment to me at first, but then I realized that it was going to serve multiple purposes. Not only was it going to show me how I read and serve as a starting point from which I could begin to improve, but it was also going to show Dr. Yancey where I stood in my development as a reader, thus giving her an idea of where I needed to go from there. It took me a little while to actually be able to write down the process of how I read onto paper, as this was something that I had never even thought about before. After some contemplation, I was able to create my own personal reading map, which explains the way that I go about understanding the material I read. Through this assignment, I began to realize much more about the way I read and interpret things. My map showed me that I read a first time, try to understand what it is saying and decide if it makes sense to me, read it a second time, summarize and interpret it, go back and interpret again, and then finally determine whether or not I like it and agree with it. I thought at the time, and still do today, that my map was a pretty good description of the way I read. If I were to create a new map today, having taken this course, I think that it would look similar to my original map; however, I would add reading the piece more than twice, more interpretations, and also discussing the piece with a peer if possible. Around the same time, we were given another assignment that helped to establish me as a reader. We were to email Dr. Yancey about the most recent book we have read, something we have read and did not like, and lastly, the type of reader that we think we are. In doing this, I came to the conclusion that I envisioned myself as the type of reader that enjoys fun and entertaining books or articles. I have had to read many serious and unhappy novels for school, which probably has a lot to do with why I do not like to read. Aside from this, only a few weeks into the semester, I had already learned more about the way I read from the assignments in this class. . . .
>
> —Harriet

The lived curriculum can be tapped through a diversity of activities that introduce the course, lead into various units within the course, and weave throughout the course.

What have I learned from tapping the lived curriculum?

1. Students like texts that teach them something: they are instrumental readers. Partly this is because they don't read much. Students do seem to have found ways to satisfy requirements (e.g., state tests) without developing the practices their grades and test scores suggest they have developed.

2. Their knowledge of literature seems to have two foundations: (a) what teachers have told them, and (b) biography. This latter—the literary text qua artist's biography—is the most common default: they assume that if they know about the writer's life, they can tease out a theme, and one theme is all, they say, they need. Literature is a perfect ratio: one text, one theme. And in many settings, it had best be the right theme.

3. Students don't read very well, nor do they have differentiated reading processes. They have been guided in their readings, and the bulk of their reading has been in textbooks they cannot mark up. Consequently, they can read, if by read we mean respond to a prescriptive set of instructions; they haven't been asked to guide their own reading, to make their own questions.

4. Students' maps of their reading show a reader's block that parallels a writer's block. Helping students "unblock" is one purpose of such a course; the map is one index to how well that process is working.

5. Students dislike texts they cannot connect to. They dislike required reading, in part because they do not know how to make it their own. When asked to make it their own, when asked real questions about it, when asked to participate in learning about their own reading, students are surprised to find they can like literature.

6. People have networks for activities they enjoy. Students go to the movies with friends; they share recommendations for music and video games. They do not have parallel networks for reading. Creating these—involving a network of authors they like and a network of fellow readers—is one way to create a reading public. Our classes can participate in this activity, but the activity needs to extend beyond our classes. Helping students identify such networks and make the transition into them is one outcome we might assign to our classes.

7. When asked about disliking texts, students can answer. Perhaps not that ironically, when they are allowed to dislike, they are more inclined to like, and both of these require judgment. The aim here is to encourage a more reflective stance, to engage in judgments that help us all think.

8. Literature has always had a social component to it; restoring that component is key.

Notes

1. In 2002 the New York Regents test received unwanted attention when it was discovered that in several of the text selections, passages had been expunged, thus linking testing with censorship.

2. At Tidewater Community College, Chris Jennings leads a FIPSE grant–funded effort intended to align curricula between the high schools in Virginia Beach and TCC, a four-sited community college in southeastern Virginia. Based on three innovations—collaborative faculty development, writing centers in the high schools, and portfolios of student work—the project has been terrifically successful. More students go on to college, get better grades once there, and stay longer. In reviewing student work, however, a continuing sticking point between the high school teachers and the college teachers is the role of student poetry in the portfolio (and thus in the curriculum), with the former valuing it highly and the latter not.

3. This is not to say that treating visual images in multiple media might not be useful, as a student explains:

> You asked me how the discussion of visual images (derived from the descriptions in texts) and their deeper meanings in my Literature class affects my understanding. I find that this kind of examination of the imagistic details greatly aids my comprehension of the issues at hand.
>
> What I was thinking when I connected this idea with this class was about the differences between what I might connect with an actual image such as a drawing or photograph and a mental image resulting from a textual description. In Literature class, for example, when we were studying *A Tale of Two Cities,* we spent a lot of time discussing the streets. I had to come to my conclusions through my reading of descriptive texts. One passage discussed the disorder of the street stones, and how they seemed to have been designed to lame all living creatures. However, a photo of an uneven street with irregular stones jutting out everywhere may not necessarily make me think of the disorder and the pain associated with the streets in the novel, but in the text, the language used is obviously foreshadowing the French Revolution and the deaths in the street.
>
> In this class, I was doing almost the opposite kind of association with my aesthetic projects. I was trying to portray aesthetically pleasing ideas through visual images rather than words. I think that by exploring both of these techniques of analysis, I can see how some ideas might be better expressed through visuals like photography or art, while others are better expressed through written text.
>
> —Kelly Baranowski

4. It's worth noting that the curricula we invent construct us as well as our students, often in surprising ways.

3 The Delivered Curriculum

One premise of the sequence of desire is that great poems deliver us to ourselves. They read us.

Edward Hirsch

In some ways, we might assume that the delivered curriculum is the "easy" curriculum, given that this is the curriculum that is visible—in syllabi, in reading and writing tasks, in course outcomes and goals. The delivered curriculum, all too often, *is* the curriculum.[1] At the same time, the delivered curriculum (over)relies on students playing a singular role: as it is conventionally played, the school game, which spins off from the delivered curriculum, asks students to tell us what they know, not what they don't know. It rewards students for strongly asserting their claims to knowledge, typically represented in a thesis-and-support format. In a literature class, in both high schools and colleges (and especially in AP classes), students write as junior experts, showing not the *possible* readings of a text, but rather *the best reading*, which is often enough a "universal" reading. And quite often, that best reading is the teacher's. As one student put it,

> In the past, I would read, at least for classes, like I would be tested on every little item in the book, and that really took a lot of the enjoyment out of the reading experience. And that is pretty much how I started the semester, trying to read and find the universal theme and trying to remember each insignificant detail because this was an English class and that is how you learn about literature; there is always a right way to read a poem, a novel, a play, etc.

In part, of course, such an attitude stems from a confusion located in genre, as suggested here: students read a work of literature as though it were a lab manual or a set of directions or a textbook, a text requiring one reading, *a right way to read*.

But such an understanding is also located in the mystery of a correct reading that has to be, as Charles D'Ambrosio notes, excavated from the text. In other words, general cultural understandings

> Like a lot of people, my father felt that a poem was a bunch of words with a tricky meaning deeply buried away, like treasure, below a surface of rhyming sounds.
> —Charles D'Ambrosio

and practices play a significant role in the approaches and attitudes students bring with them to literature class. I'd like to mark two. First, in general, reading literature—and in particular, poetry—is understood as an esoteric and mysterious activity. Second, schools themselves perpetuate such an understanding. Consider, for instance, how most English teachers read a text they enjoy: with pen/highlighter/pencil in hand. Most teacher-readers have a system of annotations to mark their readings: arrows to other points, highlighting in different colors, underlining and circling and writing their own texts in the margins; all of these marginalia talk with and talk back to the text being read.

> The biggest annoyance of the book is that the page margins are too narrow. When I read a book, I read with a pencil in my hand. I also encourage my students to do the same so that they can fully engage with the content. In this book in particular, readers need room to raise questions, insert comments, and explore possible applications. (Roen, 115)

The idea of talking back to books is such a critical piece of our understanding that we often talk about curriculum itself as a conversation (Applebee), and we mean it as more than a metaphor. Students, on the other hand, have to do such markings—if at all—in their heads or on another sheet of paper. Why? Because they *return their books:* schools want to recycle books, so high school students are required to return them in pristine condition. *Unmarked.* When students head off to college, they bring the same practice with them, this time justifying it by the higher price a used book will bring if it too returns unblemished. If students are conversing with these texts, they are doing so silently—and invisibly. It's possible, of course, that students are conversing but that their conversation is simply not represented on the page. Still, representing, I want to claim, matters. More than this, representing how you read, how you *come to understanding*—that's a (first) goal of any literature class.

> Although this book is a gift, we have some requests of you: We ask that you not only explore the book, but . . . [p]ersonalize your book. Mark words and passages. Draw figures around certain parts of the text that you like. . . .—From the wrap on a book given to all Virginia Tech First-year students in August 2002

The first formal assignment in my class (see Figure 3.1) is twofold:

1. not-understanding and
2. understanding.

Assignment One: English 202

The purpose of this assignment is for you to show that you understand how to read poetry, how to interpret poetry in a number of ways, and how to explain that to others. Everyone has the same first step: explain what you don't understand in a poem in three moves:

Identify the poem and summarize it.

Explain where you get lost/what you don't understand.

Raise other questions about the poem.

In helping your colleague understand the poem, write a response (in the form of a letter if you like) that helps him/her read the poem and understand it better. You may find the following structure useful:

Introduce the poem and describe what the writer doesn't understand.

Provide a summary of the poem.

Provide one interpretation of the poem.

Provide a second interpretation of the poem.

Explain how these interpretations respond to the writer's confusion.

Express a preference for one interpretation (optional).

Figure 3.1

What happens when we change the school game by asking students to begin by marking—or mapping—what they don't understand? In other words, suppose that in approaching poetry, we focus on understanding writ plural:

what we do understand

what we don't understand

how we could understand

how we grow in understanding

how we decide what understandings are possible

Exploring understanding through identifying and representing what we don't understand can be viewed through two related conceptual frames: palimpsest and palimtext. *Palimpsest,* as Michel de Certeau explains in *The Practice of Everyday Life,* refers to a kind of representation that the map pretends to. Mapmaking itself is exemplar par excellence of representation. As we know, maps seek through one or more devices to stabilize a fluid and dynamic space, and most if not all of us have benefited from their efficacy in so doing. Given the intent of helping someone locate a place in an unknown environment, be it real, like a geographical place, or conceptual, like a curriculum, such stabilization has much to recommend it. At the same time, of course, such a stable representation typically and fundamentally misrepresents the thing represented. As the example of the Mercator map attests, we live in a world shaped by such misrepresentations; they are ubiquitous, and we are impervious.

Seeking a radical design practice that would permit representation of multiplicity in maps of various kinds—territory, socioeconomic distribution, political conflicts, identifying symbolism and the like—de Certeau found in palimpsest a new semiotic, a new means of showing the "imbricated strata" inherent in any space a map might mark. The space itself, according to de Certeau, *is* a palimpsest, which only becomes obvious if and when the means of representation are likewise multiple. Taking a cue from de Certeau, Barton and Barton have discussed layering as one method for accomplishing a fuller representation. We might see this in multilayered maps of the world; we might see this in multilayered X-ray maps used to diagnose cancer and other diseases; we might see this in layered interpretations of a poem that collectively function to map its possibilities.

More recently, literary theorist Michael Davidson has talked about what he calls the role of *palimtext*—a specifically verbal instantiation of palimpsest—in understanding any given work of an artist. He claims:

> The palimtext is neither a genre nor an object, but a writing-in-process that makes use of any number of textual sources. As its name implies the palimtext retains vestiges of prior writings out of which it emerges. Or more accurately, it is the still-visible record of its responses to earlier writings. (78)

According to Davidson, reading a text in its own context—that is, reading it as a palimtext—is a best way of reading precisely because of the multiplicity made possible.

Just as important, both of these—palimpsest and palimtext—speak to the shifting relationships between context and text: they understand context not as separate from text, or as a place from which textual meaning evolves, but rather as *a part of* text. This sense of context—including the not-understandings and the understandings and the interpretations—is the space in which meaning is created.

In class, students begin mapping understandings, each student identifying a poem she or he likes, one disliked, and one not understood. The aim is triple: more careful readings; a record of those readings; an exchange with one another about those readings. A classroom intertext, reading made social.

James begins:

1. I really enjoyed reading the poem <u>Evolution</u>, by Sherman Alexie. I liked it because it's easy to understand and fun to read. It talks about how Buffalo Bill opened up a pawn shop, bought the Indians possessions until the Indians had pawned all they had including their hearts, and then he repaints his sign to say "The Museum of Native American Cultures." It is pointing out how fake the white man's portrayal of Native American Culture/history is.

2. I disliked the poem <u>Oread</u>, by H.D. I didn't like it because it seemed like something anyone can throw together. I didn't see any beauty or skill in it what-so-ever. It just seems to be talking to the sea and at the same time describing it.

3. A poem I didn't understand is r-p-o-p-h-e-s-s-a-g-r, by e.e. cummings. It has crazy symbols, punctuation, and parenthesis at random. I can make out some words in it, but not enough to know what it is about or why it's written so crazily.

We begin to explore what we don't understand. The beginnings are brief glances, punctuated by frustration. Students don't know where or how to begin.

> The poem I do not really understand is Robert Lowell's "Skunk Hour." I just do not understand how any of it fits together.
> —Stacey

Not-understanding is not an absence, but rather an acquired art. As students learn, articulating what they don't understand is a critical first move toward a fuller, more complex understanding. As they begin, students often revert to a familiar default that saves them from reading the poem and from not understanding: If only they knew about the poet's life, they would know the poem.

> Before we can understand the poem "Genuis Child," we need to know more about the author, Langston Hughes.
> —Bret

We return to the poems and read them as far as we can. We start with what we *do* understand, spending the time we otherwise might have spent asserting that we can't understand in mapping what we read, taking the poem as far we can, and then trying to see how and why we get derailed.

The poem "Zen Americana," by Paula Gunn Allen is problematic to me. I really do not know what "Zen" is, therefore I am confused from the title right to the body of the poem. I realize that the pronoun "un" means without, but the "un" world created by the poet can not possibly exist. It is difficult to understand if the speaker in the poem is trying to bring the reader into his/her world or if this is a fictional description. "Un" is repeated throughout the poem, but I do not understand why. I do not get what the poem is trying to say or what it means.

—Seema

We model a not-understanding process in class, using Robert Frost's "Design." We read recursively and talk about such readings explicitly: there is a *language of reading* that accompanies process. We go line by line, moving forward, then shifting back to see how earlier lines read in the context of later lines. We talk about how to make sense of a poem.

Often students find in *questions* a place to begin not understanding:

In Just
The poem I chose that was confusing was In Just, by E.E. Cummings. The poem is set in the spring time. I know this much because Cummings directly mentions the spring and refers to it as "when the world is mud," meaning when the dirt turns to mud because of the spring rain. "When the world is mud," seems like a very bleak way to describe spring time, which is usually characterized by the soft rain, singing birds, and blooming flowers. In the poem, there is a balloon man who whistles and two sets of friends come running (Eddie & Bill, and Betty & Isabel). The boys were playing with marbles, and the girls were playing hop-scotch and jump rope. The part I don't understand is about the balloon man. I don't know what a balloon man is. I think if I understood what a balloon man was, and the meaning of the title "in Just," I might have a better idea of what point the poem is trying to get across. Maybe he makes balloon animals?

"The world is puddle-wonderful," this line seems to be referring to spring as a wonderful "puddle" as opposed to "when the world is mud," mentioned in the first line of the poem. I don't understand what seems to be a change in the poet's mood. Maybe he was being sarcastic. Why is the balloon man queer? Why is the balloon man "goat-footed"? Why does the balloon man whistle "far and wee"? And why do the children come running when he does so? The poem is short, so the poet has to make every line significant in order to get the point across. However, there are many lines that I don't quite understand the meaning of. I attribute my inability to decipher the poem to my lack of knowledge of what a "balloon man" is. The reference to goat-footed could be some reference to Satan. Satan is often depicted as half man, half goat because he was derived almost completely from the Greek pastoral deity Pan (who was half man, half goat). Also, in the dictionary, one definition for the word "just" states: "*Archaic* Righteous in the sight of God." So perhaps there are some religious interpretations that are over my head, but where in the world does the balloon man fit in? I have no clue what a balloon man is or why he would be symbolic of Satan. E.E. Cummings is just a weird poet anyway. I have never really been able to understand his poems, and this poem is no exception.

—James

James works in multiple contexts:

- *What he knows to be true*—"I know this much because Cummings directly mentions the spring and refers to it as 'when the world is mud,' meaning when the dirt turns to mud because of the spring rain."
- *What he believes to be true*—"E.E. Cummings is just a weird poet anyway."
- *What he researches*—"in the dictionary, one definition for the word 'just' states: '*Archaic* Righteous in the sight of God.'"
- *What he cannot make sense of*—"Why is the balloon man 'goat-footed'?"

The movement to not-understanding is characterized by

1. Understanding-what-it-is-possible-to-understand
2. Genuine questioning located in the context of understanding
3. Dissonance about the poet

The dissonance, of course, if left unquestioned, provides a rationale for *never* understanding.

Students begin to map contradictions, seeing in them a place for not-understanding. They begin by asserting that a poem is confusing, using that confusion as a point of departure, a claim. The context of life in southern United States, for instance, here provides the background against which the poetic text is plotted:

Night, Death, Mississippi, pg 274 This poem is confusing. In the first stanza there is a sound like someone is screeching. It could be a bird or a person and an old, smelly, thin man hears it and laughs. He goes to the porch to listen in the "windowless night." I don't understand the symbolism here. Be there with Boy and the rest is the next line. Boy is capitalized so I assume that is a name for the boy. "Time was. Time was. White robes like moonlight in the sweetgum dark." I am lost on the symbolism here too. White

robes like the KKK? The poem goes on to talk about cutting
something off of Boy who has groinfire. "Time was. A cry?" Boy
deserves a drink when he gets home. In the second part of the
poem the narrator switches. He is talking about beating someone
and in between each stanza there is a sentence that seems to be
the opposite mood of the other lines. The narrator keeps changing
and you never know who is talking. It is very sporadic. The poem
says something about the KKK. I can't tell the meaning. Is this
person feeling bad about what the KKK does or are they for it? I
can't tell. The images seem to want to make you sympathetic to the
KKK members, but they are really terrible people.

—Natasha

Students begin to explore. They don't have to have the answers,
not at first. They can help one another. In fact, they *have* to help one
another; they have to read together. After rehearsals, the random, frustrated "But I don't understand" has taken a new form: an informed request for assistance in reading.

Dear Classmate, I am having a bit of trouble understanding a
poem and would like your help. The poem is on page 93 of the
text book and is titled *Pied Beauty* by Gerard Manley Hopkins.
There are several elements that make this poem difficult to understand. Structure, content, images and sounds all make this poem
difficult. The structure of this poem is somewhat different. It is not
divided into specific stanzas, to me it appears choppy and unorga-
nized. What direction does the poet want the audience to take
when reading this poem? Is the structure meant to be apart of the
beauty? The content and images present in the poem are also
difficult to understand. What do "skies of couple-color" and "a
brinded cow" have in common? Are they both supposed to be
images of beauty? I do not understand what Hopkins is describing.
In the second half of the poem, adjectives flow with no nouns to
say what they are describing. I am unclear about what the following lines are describing: (1) "And all trades, their gear and tackle
and trim." and (2) "All things counter, original, spare, strange."
What exactly do they have to do with beauty? Or is this Poem
even about beauty? I just can not seem to understand what this
poem is trying to say or what it means. Please help me uncover it.

We are still *excavating,* but we begin to explore and we begin to pose
alternatives, to raise questions related to meaning. We consider possibilities. We locate another site of not-understanding: within the contradictions *inside* the poem.

I found the poem, The White Lilies on page 426 challenging. As
the poem begins in the first stanza, it starts out happy with images

like stars and garden with a man and a woman. Love comes to my mind. Then in the second stanza the poem takes a twist from "lingering summer evenings" to cold evening of "terror." What does the couple have to be frightened from? Maybe the feeling of love ending? Why would the author speak of devastation? The images which become unclear at this point are rising narrow columns and churning sea of poppies (what is that anyway?). In the last stanza it seems like the author becomes the man or women in the poem and tells his beloved to hush. Then the author speaks of dying which relates to white Lilies which represents death. Could it be that the couple has loved and died throughout the poem? Is it about losing your significant other? I do not understand why the author has chosen to pick death

> **The White Lilies**
>
> As a man and woman make
> a garden between them like
> a bed of stars, here
> they linger in the summer evening
> and the evening turns
> cold with their terror: it
> could all end, it is capable
> of devastation. . . .
> —Louise Glück

and love and happiness—they are contradictory images, which confuse me on the theme of the poem. Images like summer evenings, gardens and stars bring joy and love, the others like terror and bury me represent death. The author speaks of spending only summers with the loved one, is the author a mistress or away at sea in battle?

We also begin exploring what interpretations are possible. Interpretation in this instance is multiple: one will not suffice. Again, we begin small.

The Road not Taken

The Road not Taken, by Robert Frost, can be found on page 64 of Vendler. This poem interests me because it concentrates on one central question. This question, directed toward the reader, asks, "Which road will you take?" The speaker recalls a choice that he has made. He had come to a fork in the road and was not sure which was the best way to travel. Both roads looked equally engaging, but one of the roads looked like it had been taken more often. Although it was a subtle difference, the speaker decided to journey the road less traveled. He knew that it was an important decision because he would probably never come back that way again. Although he took a chance by "going against the flow" he has no regrets. He is glad that he chose to go the way that he did.

This poem may be interpreted two different ways. The speaker could have come to a physical fork in the road where he was forced to make a decision about his destination. Also, though, the speaker may have been confronted with an internal, perhaps a moral, conflict. The choice that he made may have affected his entire life. Although he chose the more difficult path, he has no regrets. If he had it over to do again, he would not change a thing. I believe that I prefer the latter interpretation because the decisions that you make, regarding your morals and standards, have the power to influence your life inconceivably.

In the next explanation, the formal one, this same student, steeped in the Bible Belt, grapples: not so much with the *how,* but with the *what:*

Mother-in-Law

There is a poem that was written by Adrienne Rich called *Mother-in-Law*. It can be found in <u>Poems, Poets and Poetry</u> on pages 212-213. Meribeth . . . , one of my classmates, expressed an interest in this work, but she did not understand every aspect. She interpreted some parts of the poem correctly, such as the fact that it is a conversational poem, but some things she did not understand. The poem does seem a bit confusing, and it took some time for me to discover what it truly meant as well.

   Mother-in Law is a conversational poem between a woman and her son's wife. The son has died leaving somewhat of an awkward relationship between the two women. Throughout the poem the two exchange dialogue. The mother-in-law begins by saying, *"Tell me something."* She is asking the daughter-in-law to tell her about her life, something that would be of interest to her. The daughter replies in lines 2-6 by listing several questions that her mother-in-law did not think to ask, questions that she would like to answer for her. These questions were, "What are you working on now, is there anyone special, / how is the job / do you mind coming back to an empty house / what do you do on Sundays." The mother-in-law simply replies with the same phrase, *"Tell me something."* Then the daughter-in-law returns with sarcastic questions, "Some secret / we both know and have never spoken? / Some sentence that could flood with light / your life, mine?" She wants the mother-in-law to really care about her life, instead of simply making casual conversation. The mother-in-law then says, *"Tell me something."* The daughter-in-law's response to the question this time is one of disgust. She recalls many times when she had tried to tell her about her life, about the many things that were going on, and the mother-in-law did not care a bit. Now that she is old she wants to hear something important before she dies, but the daughter-in-law does not care to share anything. So the mother-in-law tries again. *"You married my son, and so / strange as you are, you're my daughter / Tell me . . . ."* With this the daughter-in-law begins to open up to her. She replies, "I've been trying to tell you, mother-in-law / that I think I'm breaking in two." This is the first real thing that she shares with her. The daughter-in-law tells her of the troubles that she feels. She tells her of how she feels that she can do all of the things that she is expected to do, but she also reveals that she is miserable because she feels that she has no freedom. The mother-in-law's response to this disclosure is, "*A cut lemon scours the smell of fish away / You'll feel better when the children are in school.*" When she hears this, the daughter-in-law realizes that she cannot talk to her. She realizes that she isn't truly listening and that nothing she says is important to her. The two exchange another set of dialogue, and then the mother-in-law says with frustration, "*Tell me! / They think I'm weak and hold / things back from me. I agreed to this years ago. / Daughter-in-law, strange as you are, / tell me something true / tell me something.*" With concurrent hope and desperation the daughter-in-law finally replies,

> Your son is dead
> ten years, I am a lesbian,
> my children are themselves.
> Mother-in-law, before we part
> shall we try again? Strange as I am,
> strange as you are? What do mothers
> ask their own daughters, everywhere in the world?
> Is there a question?
> Ask me something.

With this last dialogue the daughter-in-law expresses that she is willing to share her life with her mother-in-law. Although they had not been able to do so before, she wants to start again. Maybe they could build a new relationship that can overcome the differences that they once could not surmount.

There are two interpretations that you may have of this poem. The first is fairly straightforward. There are two women who have been joined only by a man. When this man dies, so does the relationship between his mother and wife. If we interpret the poem this way, then the reason that the women do not speak, or even get along, is because they have no connection. There is nothing that holds them together, and they are not unhappy about this. They simply do not care.

There is a second interpretation of this poem. The mother-in-law and daughter-in-law did have a relationship, even a friendship, at one time. They were obviously connected through the husband/son, but they developed a bond as well that did not include him, a sincere friendship and appreciation for each other. But after the son died something happened to the daughter-in-law.

> She became a lesbian. This was something that the mother-in-law could not accept. The two began to see less and less of each other, and before long they never even talked. The relationship was ruined because the mother-in-law was unable to tolerate the fact that her friend had become a lesbian. By the end of the poem the daughter-in-law has presented her with a question. She wants to regain the friendship they once had. She wants to know if it is possible to start again. I believe that this is the interpretation that I prefer. I think that they did have a relationship at one time and that they would both like to rekindle that friendship if at all possible.

The ability to articulate not-understanding as a vehicle to understanding doesn't develop in a pattern this linear, of course, despite what this chapter suggests. What this map of such progress tries to do is represent what is possible when not-understanding precedes and is linked to understanding.

A colleague, Chidsey Dickson, e-mails me to describe an adaptation of this approach. It's another variation on the theme of not-understanding as a means to understanding.

> I'm teaching a 20th C Amer. Lit this summer and have tried out your prompts to get students thinking about [what they do and don't understand]:
>
> Summarize poem. What do you understand about it & What do you not understand? This worked . . . as you suggested: to get people to understand that the point of entry into poetry is 1. through what eludes our immediate uptake of sense and 2. dialogue—burke's "conversation." I had them exchange index cards [on which they had written their responses] and solve each other's riddles. We went around the room and almost all said that in clearing up another person's ambiguity, they found insight into their own.
>
> The pedagogical problem then for me was how to bring in discussions/vocabularies . . . into the peer "intra"-pretations? So, . . . I had them flip their index cards and identify the poem's "devices." And also for "aural/visual impressions"—metaphor and metonym (the latter I defined semiotically as Brummet does in Rhetoric of Pop Culture: so a metonym might be the characteristic speech pattern/slang of a group). So, on the back they identify the poem's devices and then I asked them to answer their own questions . . . using what they now understood about the poem's HOW. It really worked. They could clear up confusion about hazy metaphors or details.

Equally interesting is Chidsey's theory as to why such an approach succeeds:

> Here's my first swipe at this: As it stands, I think the . . . prompt helps students to a Formalist reading of poetry. The poem is significant because it defamiliarizes—because it cleverly twists and obscures language so that it suggests some new idea about some aspect of experience. So, I told them that their Critical Reading Journals should touch on three concepts: devices, question/issue (what topic/situation the writer addresses), and significance (why the critic thinks this poem is worth attending to). The last two are hermeneutically bound up, as [Terry] Eagleton . . . makes clear. So, while students will still begin every reading, as you suggest, looking for their own connection to the work, they will work out towards a connection to a critical conversation. While the question/issue they first identify might have more to do with idiosyncrasy (or the politics of their own location), as they try on (in Montaignean fashion) one or two critical angles, they work towards connecting the personal with the political. Or something like that. . . .

Constructing a reading is an act of invention: the reflective act of mapping not-understanding begins to make such invention possible. As we have seen, such an understanding is located in close reading, association, multiple contexts, possibilities.

Students choose the poems they will read; although they are required to find certain kinds of poems—ones they like, ones they don't understand—they behave as readers in sorting through poems, finding (as do we all) ones they like, ones they don't. Often, given our anthology, with its hundreds of pages of poems tucked in the back for perusal, students choose poems I have never read. Some poems are canonical, others not. We read the poems together, read together through them again, and try to make sense of them—in the same way we might go to a film together—enjoying a text, thinking about it, attempting interpretations, constructing a reading. Admittedly, students are obligated to make *some* sense of the poem, but in addition to writing to me, they are making some sense for someone more important, someone-else-who-is-not-the-teacher: a classmate. Put differently, the assignment asks students not to write to a teacher-expert but to a colleague, one who genuinely cannot understand the poem but who has provided a beginning for understanding by articulating what is understood and, as precisely as possible, what is not. The student then replies, often in the context of discussing the poem with others. This is a palimtextual reading, an act of invention that is social.

What do I hope from such an assignment?

That students read poetry. Voluntarily.

That students make connections to poetry.

That students read poetry in an informed and confident way.

In these terms, I think this approach succeeds, and perhaps more useful, I've discerned five promising practices growing from the approach, practices that students developed without suggestion from me. They are, in fact, the practices of readers:

1. As the course proceeded, *students referred back to poems that seemed to relate to later curricular thematic issues and brought the poems forward into the discussion in appropriate ways.* For instance, when, later in the term, we read *House of Mirth* and *Invisible Man,* we discussed both in terms of the theme of invisibility. One student created a PowerPoint slide animating her sense of invisibility: she connected Robert Hayden's poem "Those Winter Sundays," which she had read earlier, with *House of Mirth.* In so doing, she created her own palimtext.

> This poem clearly shows how invisibility can be negative. The effort that his father contributed to the family was unappreciated; he was invisible to his son and his family. His family is blinded by selfishness. On this cold winter Sunday the father's love is being taken for granted. The son never realized how much his father really did for him until it was too late. He took for granted the hard work and long hours that the father contributed. One similarity between this poem and the novel *The House of Mirth,* by Edith Wharton is that the father is invisible. Just as Lily's father is invisible to her, so is the father invisible to the son in the preceding poem.

2. *Many students used a poem or a poet as an intellectual touchstone throughout the course; they saw the text or the figure as providing a developmental index: unable to provide a reading early on, they could do so now.* James, whom we met earlier, found in e. e. cummings such a touchstone:

> This classwork assignment really helped clear a lot of stuff up about myself. I not only learned what I liked, disliked, and didn't understand—but also WHY I liked, disliked, or didn't understand them. Talking about the poem I didn't understand helped me see how I read poetry and also helped me to try and get better at understanding the certain types of poetry that are confusing to me. Throughout the class I would talk about e.e. cummings' poems as

being confusing and esoteric. I think that by now I have a somewhat better understanding of his work. . . .

3. *When explaining a poem to a colleague, students theorized about how they
read, often making comparisons that allowed them to translate the new practices, the unfamiliar, into the familiar.* To cite just a few examples:

> e. e. cummings has set up a code that does need to be cracked, as
> you mentioned, in order to grasp the full meaning or meanings of
> the poem. I believe that he has set up what seems to be an impos-
> sible code, so that you, the reader, can deal with the words word
> by word in some kind of a visual sense.

Literature is kind of like reading into a mirror, the only answer that is found is through the person reading the words.	and	You were right when you said that the longer you look at the poem and the more you read over it, the more you pick up, much like those personalized license plates.

4. More generally, *in discussing a specific poem, students took on the role of
teacher, theorizing about poetry in ways that made sense.*

> Poetry can have absolutely no structure at all and not give a single
> hint as to what the meaning could be. It can also have a structure
> that can be a whole meaning in itself that is totally different from
> what the words point to. This makes literature different from all
> kinds of texts because it forces the reader to think about what the
> words mean.

5. Not least, *students found that poetry meant something—to them—and they
shared this experience with others outside the class.* Perhaps most profound
was the note placed inside her portfolio by a student:

> A personal note to Kathleen Yancey
> This poem by William Wordsworth touches me close to the heart,
> because it is one of my Father's favorites. He is a man whom I
> greatly admire for all he accomplishes in life. Throughout my life,
> he has been my inspiration to succeed. And though we have few
> conversations, his love for flowers is something which brings us
> together. Waking up early Sunday mornings, I help him in the
> garden and can feel the mutual satisfaction by a smile on his face.
> This poem reflects independence and love for simplicity, which is
> something my Father has passed onto me.

Asking students to explore not-understanding as a means of under-standing asks students implicitly to develop a reading process. More-over, this process becomes generalized as students work through close readings of individual poems; as they choose their touchstone poems; as they, in a Vygotskian move, explain to others that which they would know themselves. A quarter of a century ago, Richard Young outlined a similar approach to developing a writing process. In opposition to those who understood writing as a solitary and random act subject only to muse and hope, Young argued the reverse: that writing is not myste-rious; that it is more than a gift or a talent; that it can be taught and learned: "The imaginative act," he says, "is not absolutely beyond the writer's control; it can be nourished and encouraged" (57). Young's fa-vored technique to help the writer was the heuristic, a set of questions intended to bring a writer to insight. In describing the value of the heu-ristic, Young also suggests the value of any technique that can be used to structure a creative act such as writing or reading:

> For to use a heuristic appropriately the writer must see the situa-tion he is confronting at the moment as a specific variant of the kind of situation for which the procedure was designed; he must behave in some sense as though he has been there before. If he regards each situation as unique, he has no reason to believe that a technique that was useful once will be useful again. (57)

The reading heuristic proposed here is basically simple: articulate what you understand; articulate what you don't and identify the contexts that help explain that not-understanding; help others to understand; help others to interpret. The reader interpreting several poems, like the writer composing several texts, may come to understand each individual act more generally, as "a specific variant of the kind of situation for which the procedure was designed." If, then, the situation and its more gen-eral features can be identified, we can employ them again to good ef-fect—as writers and, by implication, as readers.

Equally important is a reader's identity. In "Hell's Bibliophiles: The Fifth Way of Looking at an Aliterate," John Ramsay writes about teaching a literature course in which instructor and students both iden-tify as readers and as nonreaders. As he notes, such an approach, be-cause of the disclosure required, relies on both "reflection and candor" (54). Many of his students—at Carleton College, an elite liberal arts in-stitution in the Midwest—are apparently like mine at this land grant university in the Southeast; they too tell an all-too-familiar story of re-membering their childhood reading fondly, in great contrast to their current reading lives. "These students," Ramsay says, "drew a sharp nostalgic distinction between the leisurely joy of reading during their childhoods and the high-stress, low-learning 'assigned reading' of high school and college" (54). Ramsay's approach, like the one outlined here, positions students not as nonreaders but as *potential readers*:

> Instead of the lack of the reading habit, it would be more accurate to talk of the "loss of the reading habit." Instead of [perceiving this loss in] "incapable readers, it would make more sense to say "in slow and frustrated readers." Instead of "who choose not to read," it would be more truthful to write "who choose to read despite feeling enormous stress, confusion, and pressure." This is [a] . . . way of looking at an aliterate—from the struggling reader's point of view. (56)

Questions provide a reason to read, and people who want to read have a reason to ask questions. As we know, the best questions are those that occur *within* the nexus of the personal and the academic. Those are the questions that motivate us; those are the questions we carry with us. We cannot find those questions for others, but we can help them find them for themselves.

Note

1. The delivered curriculum, of course, is constituted by all the components of the class; the syllabus, the activities, the formal assignments, and so on. It is, I hope, clear that we are reading a good deal of poetry of various kinds in addition to several novels, chapters from self-selected books, drama, and so on. In this chapter, then, I focus on adding the role of *not* understanding to the delivered curriculum, and on how that changes the delivered. Of course, seen another way, the entire project is about changing the delivered curriculum.

4 The Experienced Curriculum: Closing the Circle

When you read my work, you may think "simile" or "metaphor," but what you really get is the storm, the dark mansion, the servant girl standing alone in Columbus Circle.

Terrence Winch

A third way of understanding curriculum is to think of it as *experienced*, what some call the de facto curriculum—that is, the curriculum that *students construct* in the context of both the lived curriculum they bring with them and the delivered curriculum we seek to share. Given the nature of reading as a constructive act, students will necessarily make what *they* will of text; although not always acknowledged, the experienced curriculum has always been part of school. In practice, however, as we saw with the lived curriculum, our recognition of curriculum other than the delivered varies. Too often we ignore the other (hooks), seeming to believe that if we focus hard enough on what *we* want students to know, our delivered curriculum will subsume or replace the lived and the experienced. In this context, it's worth noting that the discipline of school, through essays and tests and grades, rewards those who are willing to have "their" curricula so erased.

> It [a poem] is not an object or an ideal entity. It happens during a coming-together, a co-penetration, of a reader and a text. The reader brings to the text his past experience and present personality. Under the magnetism of the ordered symbols of the text, he marshals his resources and crystallizes out from the stuff of memory, thought, and feeling a new order, a new experience, which he sees as the poem.
> —Louise Rosenblatt

Still, the study of literature isn't a unified construct. In some situations, we not only include the experienced curriculum but also specifically invite and theorize it as a form of delivered curriculum. This is one way to understand reader-response pedagogies, in which responding to and interpreting the experienced reading serves as one if not the principal goal of the course. In still other cases, we devise an approach—as do Robert Scholes and

Gerald Graff—that connects the lived curriculum of student experiences, such as those with rock music, with those of literature precisely to link the two, using each to make sense of the other. Put succinctly, we aren't consistent about the role the experienced (or the lived) curriculum might play in the delivered curriculum of school literacy.

My sense of, interest in, and exploration of the experienced curriculum grew from my curiosity about how certain activities were (or were not) working for students, and from my sense that reflection offers a powerful vehicle for inquiring into that question. I knew from reading portfolios and their reflective texts—letters and essays, annotations on individual pieces of work, sometimes collages—that students often constructed an experience different from the one (I'd thought) we'd communally shared (Yancey 1997). This observation also corresponded with research showing that students learn as much from one another as they may learn from teachers. And as a teacher steeped in writing and rhetoric, I'm familiar and comfortable with pedagogies located in principles of active learning. Such an approach allows me to learn as well. To illustrate, here I focus on a quick class activity demonstrating three related concepts that are central to the experienced curriculum in the literature class: active learning, collaborative performance, and reflection.

Like Chuck Schuster, I use reader's theater as a way to both introduce poetry and engage students. As it sounds, *reader's theater* is a performance of a text. The performers might focus on key words, highlighting those in chorus. The performers might focus on alternating or juxtapositioned voices in a text, performing those so as to draw attention to the conflicts within or the ambiguity of a text. The performers might stage a "play" of the text.

As I use this exercise, its purpose and design are quite simple. The purpose is, first, to engage students in working together to share a poem with the class, and second, to show them that the same poem can have many legitimate interpretations. To ensure that the class sees the same poem performed more than once, and thus that we have illustrated the concept of interpretation, I offer

> *Poetry teachers, especially at the high school and undergraduate levels, should spend less time on analysis and more on performance.* Poetry needs to be liberated from literary criticism. Poems should be memorized, recited, and performed. The sheer joy of the art must be emphasized. The pleasure of performance is what first attracts children to poetry, the sensual excitement of speaking and hearing the words of the poem. Performance was also the teaching technique that kept poetry vital for centuries.
> —Dana Gioia, *Can Poetry Matter?*

only two poems: Edgar Allan Poe's "Annabel Lee" and Gwendolyn Brooks's "We Real Cool." Although both are narrative poems, they (seemed to me to) offer different opportunities for performance. Additionally, most of the students tend to know the Poe and most do not know the Brooks, so there is the chance to work with both familiar and unfamiliar material. And although each term I expect students to tell me that reader's theater is yesterday's fish wrap, to date that hasn't happened. As for performance, I explain that students might see the poem as a play, complete with props and costumes; students might voice parts of speech within a poem to emphasize different themes; students might think of the poems in terms of the visual.

I ask students to choose one poem to work with, and, as I have learned, about half the students choose one, the other half of the class the other, so each poem gets "equal time" and is performed several times. Based on their preferences, I then put students in groups of three to four, giving them a short amount of planning time so they can begin to organize for their performances the next class period; the homework is for them to arrive in class prepared to perform.

Each term I see new performances of each poem. Last term, "Annabel Lee" was for one group a play, with a silent narrator sitting at a table in the dark, writing—presumably "Annabel Lee"—by candlelight, against a digital background showing a raven; two women read the poem to the audience in a kind of unconscious imitation of Thornton Wilder's stage manager narrator in "Our Town." The previous term the poem "Annabel Lee" was read by one man standing at the front of the room; at the same time, each of four women stood in a corner of the room sounding the phrase "Annabel Lee" from one corner to the next around the room in a ghostly, ongoing, not-quite-background chorus. "We Real Cool" last term was a silent video, taped at the local high school, showing a group of kids moving from opening happy stanza scene to less happy scene to unhappy scene to desperate final scene, cumulatively suggesting the different forms that "quiet lives" of desperation can take, even when "cool." The term before, "We Real Cool" was a rap, complete with in-

> Performance is the mode of communication that moves poetry from a quiet experience between a reader and a page to an interactive experience between a poet and an audience. Performance poetry can, ultimately, lead students back to the page, though when they return to the page they return with a way of reading that allows them to hear and see and feel and *do* the poem differently.
> —Lindsey Ellis, Anne Ruggles Gere, and L. Jill Lamberton

struments, pool cues, and shades, each student singing a stanza, the full poem repeated several times, each rendition more energetic than the last, the iterations increasingly ironic, the iteration culminating in a final choral rendition of "We die soon."

I knew that the student performances helped me understand the poems differently. The sadness and irony of "We Real Cool" seemed almost inevitable: *was that the point?* Previously, the love expressed in "Annabel Lee" was to me more real life than paranormal; after that chorus, I wasn't so sure. *What is the nature of love?* I knew what I'd learned in watching. What, I wondered, had students learned? Having seen different "versions" of a poem, how did *they* understand it now? What was the effect of creating a performance based on their understanding of that specific poem? What had they learned about poetry more generally in the process of *creating* the performance? To find out, I simply asked.

"How do you see these poems now?"

> The poem Annabel Lee is made up of love, life, and death, and it may be interpreted differently by different people. Three groups seemed to do the same idea of having 3 different people read of the three (love, life, death); many of the lines were the same, but others varied. Just because one person may think one thing and another may think something else, you wonder if those ideas are what the author wanted each reader to understand or is there another interpretation that no one has yet seen/interpreted.
>
> —Amanda

"And what did you learn about poetry in the process of creating a performance and of seeing the performances of others?"

What students say they learn in this exercise varies by student. Sometimes they learn that poetry reads differently when read aloud. Sometimes they learn that literature wants to be read by people together as much as or more than by people alone. Sometimes they learn that the same poem can be read in completely different ways by people who seem very similar. Sometimes they learn how to explain better why they read the poem the way they do as they talk back and forth about what and how it seems to mean, especially as they try to figure out how to design a reader's theater performance.[1]

This last "learning"—*how to explain better why they read the poem the way they do as they talk back and forth about what and how it seems to mean, especially as they try to figure out how to design a reader's theater performance*—seems particularly important to many students: this is not the way (they say) they have read poetry before. Just as important, it's directly connected to the task. In the task—present the poem—students face an exigence, which is to perform the poem in some way, and they know that to create a performance of it, understanding it is a first step. Equally (or perhaps more) significant is the audience for this performance: their peers. Because the assignment is not graded—and that fact is worth repeating: this is an ungraded, informal exercise—the motivation is intrinsic and social, located in the students' working together and presenting to peers. In a culture of high-stakes testing, these stakes (ironically) are perhaps the highest. Not least, the reflection that concludes the exercise follows principles of good practice: it comes after a communal experience and asks students to articulate that experience by (1) focusing on a specific instance, (2) explicating it, and (3) working toward generalization. Overall, the assignment invites individual interpretation within the context of the explicitly social.

Partly, of course, this articulation of how such an assignment works is *my* interpretation, but it is based on what students like Lance report, as well as on what I see in their performances and their continuing work with literature. As Lance relates,

> At first I was really confused about some of the lines. "We jazz june" was really hard to understand at first. We sat down for a long period of time and broke each line into different scenes which helped me understand the poem better. The representation that I got was the type of kids in our video living wild lifestyles and dying at a young age.
>
> [A]t first I hated it [reading poetry]. But making this video made it fun. We had a good time while trying to learn what the poem was about, which was something I never would have thought would happen. I think I will understand it easier now by just breaking it down into each individual line and then slowly piecing it back together.

This is the hope of a reflective curriculum: that the processes students engage in while "trying to learn what the poem [is] about" are processes that will reflectively "transfer" as they read and seek to understand other poems, and that these processes, such as "breaking it down into each individual line and then slowly piecing it back together," are ones they will then use on their own.

In his portfolio reflection at the end of the term, Lance returns to the role this exercise played in helping him learn. He links the performance experience with the communal task as he places it in his autobiographical (lived curricular) context:

> Poetry up until this class I had given up all hope on. I always hated it because it seemed to me that if I didn't see a poem the way my teachers did, I was completely wrong, and this made me feel stupid and helpless when it came to interpreting it. I always have enjoyed plays. I guess the way we kind of performed plays in English classes entertained me more than being told to read it on my own. Getting to see the play acted out always made it easier to understand and more meaningful to me.

The key here seems to be that in performing the play, Lance is removed from what it is he thinks school requires—trying to produce the "teacher's" prior meaning, which ultimately makes him feel "stupid and help- | I never strike a false note. | less." Instead, through the assignment of | —Winch | performance, he has permission to create his own meaning. This accounts in part for why reader's theater (and similar activities) is attractive to students—that and the fact that they create this performance *together:*

> The fact that we sat down with each other in my group and broke each line up, really helped me understand something about poetry in general.

Working as members of a *we*, students engage in processes they can use on their own, and in accounting for their activity in a reflection, they articulate the experienced curriculum.

Another kind of assignment—this one more elaborated and formal, culminating in a graded essay—also asks students to articulate the experienced curriculum, this time by making the experienced curriculum visible through the vehicle of the "pop-up": it's the pop-up literature assignment. A *pop-up* refers to a specific kind of intertextuality, the kind we see, for instance, in music videos in which cartoon bubbles have been inserted so that new information can be displayed as the video proceeds, and more recently (and annoyingly) to the advertisements that "pop up" on Web pages. A song by Jewel thus includes in the many pop-ups the fact that she lived in a car for a year, that most people don't live in cars, and that she is a writer as well as a songwriter. Seen one way, of course, a pop-up is merely an intertextual exercise, each pop-up bubble a connection to a contextual element outside a central text. We might, then, consider a set of pop-ups the way we consider the endnotes in this chapter: they extend and comment on texts. In this iteration, however, they *visualize* both the delivered and the experienced curriculum. And pop-ups work differently also, especially when electronic, through

Literature Pop-up Presentation
Or: Using Several Contexts to Make
Sense of a Novel
Yancey/Spring 2003

The Task

Help the class understand the novel
by connecting it to/reading it through
multiple contexts

Epic	Norris
Romance	History of the railroads
Gothic	California history
Western	Naturalism

The Team

See assignment sheet

The Schedule

Tues, 2/18	Discuss Task
	Develop Schedule
	Planning Doc (PD)
Tues, 2/25	Presentation

The Conference

Week of 3/4

The Presentations

See evaluation sheet

Parameters of the Presentation

include a focus: at the end of the
presentation, our classmates will
understand what about the novel?

include some (quick) summary of the
novel

include some connection to the
contexts

include at least one visual: overhead?
poster? video clip? PowerPoint? Web
page?

medium-invested mechanisms for extension, for elaboration, and (most important) for surprising effects. As Anne Aronson explains,

> I am alternately amazed, intrigued, and entertained by the ever-expanding interplay of word and image around me. My favorite example of this interplay is the show "Pop-Up Video" on VH1, the music video alternative to MTV. The show, which has become increasingly popular, is similar in format to other music video shows, except that the visual/musical presentation is interrupted by as many as 25 bubbles of text which "pop up" on the screen. The text bubbles provide a kind of "reading" of the video, offering interpretations of themes and artifacts in the video, fragments of musical history, and morsels of music world gossip. In the pop-up version of "Closing Time," for example, we learn where the video was shot, who is dating whom in the video, and how the writer got the idea for the song. The bubbles are interesting in that they disrupt the familiar genre of the music video, creating an odd hybrid of comic strip, celebrity gossip column, trade magazine, and pop culture criticism. Pop-up videos bracket the video, denaturalize it, force us to think about it as a medium. They are striking examples of how music, image, spoken language, and writing can converge. (n. pag.)

As a device, pop-ups are attractive textually because of their linkage of form and material: they are directly linked to a primary text, and that linkage permits a full range of "quotations" of other contexts, ranging from the ridiculous to the sublime. Pop-ups can link to other literature, to background information and associations, to contemporary juxtapositions. Collectively, pop-ups on or in a single text can create a random metatext, and it is equally possible that collectively pop-ups can create a series of parallel texts, or, perhaps, multiple stories prompted by, but not necessarily limited to, a "primary" text. And, as Aronson notes, pop-ups allow both composer and consumer to engage in intellectual *interplay* of both visual and verbal varieties. Cognitively, pop-ups are attractive because they allow the (new) composer to use the primary text as a way of engaging with and thus generating new material, which in Kressian terms can be an exercise in design as well as in critique. In the term of Jay David Bolter and Richard Grusin, pop-ups permit a kind of *re-mediation* of the original text: through the addition of pop-ups, new connections and thus new knowledge are made. Cartographically, pop-ups are attractive because they permit composers to map immediate and indirect connections and implied and potential relationships. When students create them without direction or censorship, they function as a kind of mapping of the experienced curriculum, a visual way of reading with/in many contexts. And when a group creates a set of pop-ups on a literary or other text, the new text locates a new reading, both individually and collectively, and helps provide a point of departure for students to try out their own mappings, their own interpretations. And in a class, pop-ups are attractive for all these reasons, *and* because they—much like and yet different from reader's theater—ask students to perform a text.

> How knowledge is acquired matters as much as what is acquired. When knowledge is acquired in service of a goal, it remains forever linked to that goal.
> —Roger Schank

My design of this assignment, however, was first motivated by more commonplace occasions: my experiences watching the VH1 program "Pop-Up Videos" with my two then-adolescent children and my reading the *New Yorker*. In February 2001, the *New Yorker* included a cartoon titled "The Norton Pop-Up Anthology of English Literature" (see Figure 4.1). Among other texts, it included a poem by John Donne: "Holy Sonnet 10." The concluding pop-up in the right margin reads, "John Donne died in 1631. He's still dead." That struck me as accurate—and funny. As I read through the other poems, I had the same reaction to the pop-ups, and I could see how students would enjoy them—and

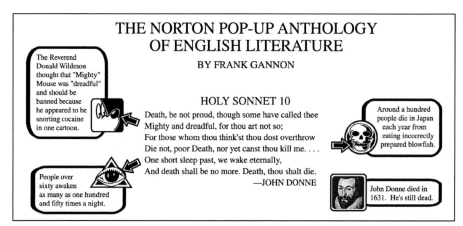

Figure 4.1

by enjoy I meant of both critique and design, of both education (Donne did die in 1631) and enjoyment (Donne is still dead). In their ability to both instruct and delight, pop-ups seemed poetic. And in the students' hands, pop-ups as performance could provide an especially interesting challenge; how do you create pop-ups that are relevant (instructing) and engaging (delightful)? In sum, I decided to create an assignment that would engage students in the same kind of activity.

As I designed the task, I found it (again) to be related to my curiosity about student learning: when I read almost any text, I seem to make multiple connections almost naturally, although I understand that such connecting is anything but natural, and I know that some of the connections are richer than others. Surprisingly—or it certainly seemed surprising once I'd thought about it—I had never asked students to record or note or make visible the connections they make when reading, assuming (often incorrectly) that students did make such notes. In asking for this pop-up palimpsest, I'd be able to see the beginning of what had heretofore been invisible. In general, too, "good" readings of texts are well connected in both quantity and

Regrettably, literature instruction is usually focused on single texts (Beach, Appleman, & Dorsey, 1994). In analyzing students' think-aloud responses to texts, Rogers (1988) discovered that a mere 1% of students make references to other texts. Only if students saw other texts as almost identical were they able to make intertextual links. The one-text-at-a-time tradition, therefore, translates beyond an isolated reading experience to an experience that reinforces a student's belief that each text is an island, that each text does indeed stand alone.—Kettel and Douglas

The Octopus as an Epic

Well, why not have a Commission of our own? Never mind how we get it, let's get it. If its got to be bought, let's buy it and put our own men on it and dictate what the rates will be.

•

Epics usually involve a hero or in this case a group of heroes banding together to fight evil. In the novel the farmers decide to get together to fight the powerful railroad. This reminded us of all of the heroes of Star Wars joining together to fight the evil Empire.

Epics usually involve a hero or in this case a group of heroes banding together to fight evil. In the novel the farmers decide to get together to fight the powerful railroad. This reminded us of all of the heroes of Star Wars joining together to fight the evil Empire.

Figure 4.2

quality: good readers make many and often highly associative connections. If indeed I wanted highly intertextual readings, perhaps this assignment would point the way toward them. And I wondered if the combined effect of pop-ups with a communal performance would make many other connections for all of us. Accordingly, I created The Pop-Up Literature Presentation, modeled on the *New Yorker* cartoon. What I intended with this presentation was simple: an opportunity for students to work in a new genre that would permit a new kind of *connectedness*, a form of knowing both tangible and symbolic. Students would, I hoped, bring their experiences to a text, connect them in multiple ways, and make the learning both visual and public for their peers in class.

The basics of my first pop-up assignment were simple: students, in groups, present a pop-up project on Frank Norris's novel *The Octopus* (see Figure 4.2). Each group chooses at least two of the eight "given" contexts—epics, naturalism, and the author himself, to name but three— for some of their pop-ups. Other contexts of their own choosing supply the rest of the pop-up linkages. After the presentations, students write an essay articulating at least three of the multiple stories of the novel. To assist students in moving from collaborative presentation to individually composed essay, I created an evaluation guide that signals the values of the project: I want the students to play with allusions, images, references, implications (see Figure 4.3)—and I want their performance to convey something about the novel.[2]

We read Frank Norris's *The Octopus* for several reasons. Since this novel isn't taught in high school, it's new to students. To date, they have not read any of Norris's work, nor is there a CliffsNotes on the novel

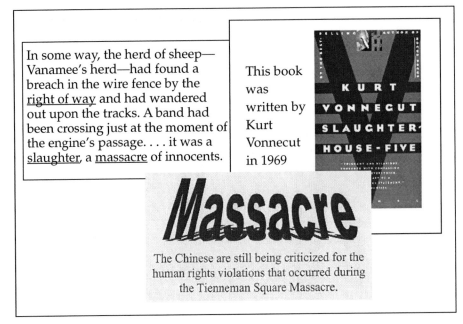

In some way, the herd of sheep—Vanamee's herd—had found a breach in the wire fence by the <u>right of way</u> and had wandered out upon the tracks. A band had been crossing just at the moment of the engine's passage. . . . it was a <u>slaughter</u>, a <u>massacre</u> of innocents.

This book was written by Kurt Vonnecut in 1969

The Chinese are still being criticized for the human rights violations that occurred during the Tienneman Square Massacre.

Figure 4.3

(although the Internet of course offers its typical mix of resources). More important, the novel lends itself to several approaches. Given its California setting and the role of the railroads, it's clearly a Western novel; given the role of Angele, the novel has elements of the gothic; given the pastoral setting and the role of the poet Presley as narrator, it's romantic; given the scope of the novel and Presley's ambition to create his own epic, it aspires to epic status. Given my interest in helping students read for different stories within a larger narrative, *The Octopus* provides an abundance of material.

Two examples suggest the kinds of approaches students take to this assignment. As we see in the planning document to the right, the script uses the *idea* of the West as a primary text and the book as supporting evidence. This group's media included e-mail, film, prior maps, and advertising. This project was more performance than presentation.

Focus:
To connect a scene from *Tombstone* (Western movie) with the spirit of the West and the history of the railroad, supported by examples from the book.
Script:
A. Show video clip from *Tombstone*.

continued

B. Rich gives an overall view of the West and what was behind the railroads in *The Octopus*, tying it to the word *money*.
C. Brian presents a pop-up off of the term *49ers*, describing the 1849 gold rush.
D. Vanessa presents a pop-up off of the word *Octopus*, describing the train itself.
E. Linda presents a pop-up off of the words *The Spirit of the West*, describing the railroad system.
F. Bobby presents a pop-up off of the word *Whiskey*, describing how the train was important in delivering it throughout the West.
G. Nikos is to perform a scene yet to be determined.
H. Tiffany presents a pop-up off of the word *Fashion*, describing what people put in their suitcases when they traveled by train.

A second project, delivered through PowerPoint, was more presentation. It used six central passages from the novel and "popped up" each of those, as we see here:

History of the Railroads passage #2 - p. 316
—will be read by Matthew and the pop-ups will be read by Nic

"You know I am one of the **lady** members of the subscription **committee** for our **Fair**, and you know we approached Mr. Shelgrim for a **donation** to help along. Oh, such a **liberal** patron, a real **Lorenzo di' Medici**. In the name of the Pacific and Southwestern he has subscribed, think of it, five thousand dollars; and yet they will talk of the **meanness** of the **railroad**."

Pop-ups (Nic)
    lady- refined and proper
    committee- group of people
    Fair- pale complexion
    donation- church offerings
    liberal- hippie or Ralph Nader
    Lorenzo di' Medici- the greatest patron of literature and art that
      any prince had ever been
    meanness- S. Bherman
    railroad- standard gauge is 4ft 8in wide

Women in the West passage - p.185
—will be read by Harriet and the pop-ups will be read by Sammy

"Annixter struck his heel into the ground with a **suppressed** oath. Always these **fool feemale women** came between him and his plans, mixing themselves up in his **affairs**. Magnus had been on the very point of saying something, perhaps **committing** himself to some course of action, and, at precisely the wrong moment, his **wife** had cut in. The **opportunity** was **lost**."

Women in the West (Harriet)

Pop-ups (Sammy)

   suppressed- hiding feelings
   fool feemale women-
      unequal treatment
   affairs- adultery
   committing- women were
      subservient to their husbands
   wife- the mother, the
      housekeeper, the cook
   opportunity- the women's
      suffrage amendment is
      introduced to the US congress in 1878
   lost- constant state of being

After the presentations conclude, I gather questions raised by the pop-up presentations. As the two sets of questions show, each term the questions vary given the experienced curriculum mapped in the pop-ups.

Term One Questions
- Is the octopus a metaphor for the railroad, the ranchers, or both? How do you know?
- One presentation emphasized that Derrick is a gambler. Do you agree? And how would you define the term *gambler* (i.e., is gambling in this sense only about money, or is it about more than/other than money)? Is your evaluation of him as a gambler important in terms of understanding *The Octopus*?
- Is one theme of the novel that it's foolish to try to get rich quick? I mean, you could make the argument that the novel is a set of textured stories about the failures that follow when people do try to get rich quickly. Do you agree?
- One presentation suggested that westerns tend to include the figure of the adventurer. If that's so, then is *The Octopus* a western? I mean, I don't see an adventurer figure here, do you? Or perhaps *The Octopus* is a Western in some ways, but not in others?
- One presentation included the idea that Presley, in trying to write his poem, needed to find or write about a "new people." Is it possible to find a new people? And if it's impossible, is that why Presley is doomed to failure?
- I'm a bit troubled by one conclusion we might draw from the novel: that the best means of survival is through the supernatural (e.g., Vanamee) or through disengagement (e.g., Presley). Is this what you read in the novel, or am I missing something?

In the first term, questions clustered around character and figure. In the second term, questions clustered around control, morality, and America. It's probably no accident that the second term was post-9/11 and the first term before it.

> Questions from Term Two
> • Are Magnus and S. Behrman opposites? How/are they different?
> • Is this a comic or tragic novel?
> • Is this a story of a corrupted American dream?
> • What's the role of control?
> • What difference does it make that Presley tells the novel? What if S. Behrman told the tale?
> • Is it possible to engage in an immoral act and not be immoral?
> • Is it easier to be honest when you have nothing to lose? Is that then not really being honest?
> • When a novel goes against the grain (i.e., goes against the genre), is [it] a better novel?
> • Is the novel a story of failed compromise?
> • Is this a David and Goliath story with a different ending?
> • Is this a particularly American story?

Students also told me in several ways how the pop-up project, with its emphasis on multiple stories, had enabled them to read and learn differently. When asked what they liked about the novel, for instance, one replied,

> I like the fact that the pop up videos are helping me see connections through characters. That helps me understand the book in some way. At first, I had no idea what an octopus had to do with the book; now after talking with the groups I can see connections through the way an octopus conserves, and [I] actually learned the habits of an octopus.

Working through the supplied pop-up contexts—such as epic—and linking those to the familiar helped students read more synthetically.

The essays that developed from the pop-up literature assignment seemed different, at least in degree, and sometimes in kind. Some students, like Bobby, liked choosing the multiple stories they'd plot; these stories connected with issues he is interested in, such as the supernatural:

> Though there are many stories woven throughout *The Octopus,* I chose to describe these three. I read into these stories more than others because they caught more of my attention. I like seeing peoples' lives change for the better, so I concentrated on Annixter's life change. I am thoroughly interested in God and the supernatural, so I was naturally drawn to the story of Vanamee and the supernatural. For the third story, one cannot help but see the way the entire novel is wrapped around the central conflict of the landowners versus the railroad. *The Octopus* is a collection of

many stories within a novel, woven around a central skeleton story of life of the western people.

Others used the novel to raise and grapple with their own unanswerable questions—which, returning to my theme of literature as gen ed, is one practice I want students to adopt and carry forward into life:

> The most important thing that I learned on this paper is the difference between moral, immoral, and amoral people. I think that I have a better grasp on what each definition truly means. I honestly never knew what the word amoral meant before I wrote this paper. I also learned how to analyze [a] novel a little bit more precisely. It helped me realize that many times literature can have multiple meanings.
>
> —Dennis

And still others, like Lori, seem to weave a more theoretical text:

> There are many other stories woven into The Octopus, but of these four, I think that the story of nature and man as a species, and the epic story are the most important. These two themes look at the big picture, albeit in two different ways. The Romantic and Gothic story is more of a separate issue that lends itself to depicting the whole of the epic. It makes the characters seem more real, and we care more about them because we feel that we know them. The corruption story helps to illustrate the idea of the survival of the fittest struggle of the nature story, that people are animals and must do whatever they have to in order to survive. The political corruption is also part of the life and times of the people, so it is also a necessary part of the epic. I think that Norris' main goals were to write an epic story, and to write one that makes people think about naturalism.

For others, this exercise provided a way into literature, a means of reflective transfer. Cade, for example, claimed that "[a]nother way that I have changed is when I read novels now I try to figure out if there are multiple stories within the main story and whether or not they change the course of the story." And still others like the social element that comes with this pop-up assignment:

> I think that I've gotten a better understanding of the literature we've studied by doing pop-ups. When I have one little understanding of material, another person who has a total different perspective can help me understand what the author may have wanted the readers to know. The design of the course has made the study of literature more interesting than I thought it would be.

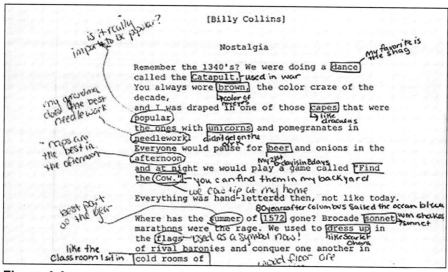

Figure 4.4

Fluent readers and synthetic readers don't need pop-ups; their imaginations and knowledge make these connections. (Which is not to say that, as the *New Yorker* cartoon illustrates, pop-ups should be confined to the weaker readers; such free association is part of the play of intellectual life.) Introducing pop-ups as a way to visualize and make social this reading process ensures that all students can participate. Or that was the hope.

The pop-up assignment had succeeded according to the terms I'd stipulated; the students made interesting connections, new questions were raised, and their essays were, I thought, more interesting and more synthesized. At the same time, I was aware that some students found it difficult to make connections with texts. Observing them working in groups as they organized for their pop-up presentations, I could see that some students made connections in a brainstorming, scattershot, confident way, while others enjoyed what their peers created but didn't participate fully. Seeking to engage all students, I thought that perhaps introducing this practice earlier might be helpful. One day early in the term, I brought in a poem by Billy Collins, who at the time was poet laureate of the United States. I asked each student to read the poem and to circle or box every connection they made while reading—whether silly, profound, interesting, or questionable—and annotate it in the margins (much like the Annotations page in *Harper's*) (see Figure 4.4). Then I asked the students to exchange poems and, in another color, to "pop up" their classmate's poem. In this way, we collected a set of individual pop-ups and a set of choral pop-ups, since some students popped up *both* the poem and the first set of annotations.[3] This is a networked reading made visible. After we completed this exercise, I took the pop-ups home and read them, marking with a yellow highlighter the ones I found intriguing, funny, smart. Each student had at least one. I arrived early for the next class period to post the pop-ups around the room, as in a gallery, and invited students to see the kinds of connections that are possible.

Not surprisingly, the better students made more connections. With practice, the weaker students become the better students.

What have I learned?

1. Students like creating pop-ups, which can take several forms: print; multimedia performance; PowerPoint presentation. In terms of student learning, is one "better" than the other? What would better be?

2. The questions raised from the patterns of the pop-ups focus class discussion on new questions. Are these the questions that students return to in their essays? In the reflective essays culminating in their portfolios?

3. Students like this kind of mapping; they share their maps. In fact, a big part of its appeal is the chance to work together *to create a new text and to perform it.* How does creating such a new text assist with understanding the old?

4. The maps reveal the issues that students care about. During the fall of 2001, the most frequent pop-up revolved around the events of 9/11: as a map of reader response, it quite visibly articulated the students' continuing concern and at the same time allowed them to see that concern as one among many. In other words, it had a relativizing effect.

5. Students who can create pop-ups make more connections, bring more contexts to bear, and read more complexly. Initially, some students aren't able to make *any* connections. They want to read for a "right" reading, or they need to know about the poet's life first, they say. Practice in this kind of reading, like other forms of reading, is an acquired art. Combining this kind of mapping of reading with a reading process map (see Chapter 2) as a social activity helps students perceive ways to read.

6. Pop-ups can show multiple stories, which helps students shift from the single thesis and support reading, so popular in many literature classes and on so many standardized tests, to a more sophisticated reading. This approach cultivates an intertext-

uality new to most students, one in which the stories of popular culture contextualize those of literature—and vice versa.
What might we learn in this process?

7. Suppose we thought of the pop-up text as the new text, the
paper itself, rather than as a rehearsal for more conventional
kinds of assignments? The pop-up text brings together a
Kressian interest in critique and design because it makes the
intersection of the lived, the delivered, and the experienced
curricula a site for a new kind of text. What might we all learn
in and through this kind of assignment? What would be the
criteria for such an assignment?

These questions—mine here and my students'—matter because
in the end, of course, curriculum is about learning, the learning that
occurs spontaneously and serendipitously, the learning that is planned,
the learning that we engage in with others.

Perhaps what I like most about the pop-up literature project is
that it emphasizes all these kinds of learnings as it brings them—and
us—together.

Notes

1. In some ways, this assignment is very like the tasks in Odyssey of the
Mind, an extracurricular effort for students in K–12 settings. Typically, students
in groups are given a task and asked to "perform" the solution to the task.
Intended both to attract creative students and to invite creativity, activities like
these belong in school as well as outside of it.

2. The evaluation form for each group is completed by all students and
passed to the group. After reviewing the response from the class, the group

Evaluation Guide Pop-Up Literature Presentations			
Outcome			
Excellent	*Strong*	*Fair*	*Poor*
Delivery			
—Focused			
—Connections from one segment to the next			
—Appropriate for audience			
Associations/Observations			
—Perceptive/insightful			
—Grounded in common texts/understandings			
—Generative (raises questions about novel)			
—Verbally illustrated/discussed			
—Visually illustrated/embodied			
Other			
—What do you understand now about the novel that you did not before?			

tallies the scores, summarizes the responses, and writes a reflection on how they will move from presentation to essay. This removes me from the process, although I read the summaries and provide feedback on them. This technique of students working with other students without teacher monitoring has been successfully applied in other contexts from biology to engineering.

3. This technique is thus very like the Web in its right and left branching; the applications of such a strategy are many. A more focused approach could prescribe certain kinds of pop-ups; a culminating poetry exercise might ask students to develop pop-ups all around the poem and readings of it, the kind of poem, and/or the poet. For a related activity, see Moran and Carson, who invite students to "make 'conversation sparks'" on sticky notes: "we push students to make a variety of types of comments that include predictions, questions, connections, clarifications, and inferences. . . ." They continue:

> We begin asking students to also jot their sparks down quickly on sticky notes before they begin talking. We've found that our students are quite open to this once they realize that it is a useful process—not just something they have to do because we said so. In their reflections, we find they internalize the importance of talking well about a novel when they are reading with a partner, book club, or full class.

Giving students the room to pause and say something about a text creates a focused opportunity to make predictions, make connections, and ask questions.

- Text-to-self connection (and then think: how does this help me understand the text better?)
- Text-to-text connection (to another book, a movie, etc.)
- Text-to-world connection
- Predictions
- Ideas for your own writing
- Advice for author
- Advice for the character
- Clarifying what the author means
- If I were the character . . .

5 Portfolios and the Representation of Student Work

We look at the present through a rear view mirror.
Marshall McLuhan and Quentin Fiore

Portfolios are commonplace in writing classes, less commonplace in literature classes. Regardless of the context, however, portfolios rely on three practices. First, students are asked to *collect* all of their work. Second, they are asked to *select* from this archive samples of work they would share with others. Third, and perhaps most important, students are asked to *reflect* on that work—to think about what they have learned, to assess which of their exhibits is the strongest and why, or to use their review of the entire portfolio to plan future activities.

Like all assessments, portfolios serve different purposes. In a class, they tend to be a vehicle for classroom learning and assessment. In cross-class or bridging contexts, as in English education courses, they work *across* classroom boundaries, attempting to show the work of each separate context as well as the links between. Within programs, they are, as David Booth argues, designed for students to connect their learnings in multiple contexts—to link what they have learned in biology, for instance, to their reading of *Frankenstein*. And still other times, as in Utah State University's English department, faculty review a subset of student portfolios for purposes of program enhancement (see Hult).

Portfolios, then, are unified as a construct. Created by the three principal activities of collection, selection, and reflection, student portfolios can be succinctly defined as collections of work, selected from a larger archive of work, on which the student has reflected. At the same time, portfolios are *rhetorical:* created in many different contexts, they can serve various purposes and speak to multiple audiences. Deciding

---

Portions of Chapter 5 have been adapted from Kathleen Yancey's article "Postmodernism, Palimpsest, and Portfolios: Theoretical Issues in the Representation of Student Work," *College Composition and Communication* 55.4 (June 2004), 738–61.

which purposes to serve and which audiences to address is an important pedagogical and intellectual task.

Given their site as a space for reflective work, portfolios seemed a desirable replacement for the end-of-term test that often concludes a literature course. By reflecting on what they had learned, how they had developed, and how they might carry forward what we had experienced, students might, I hoped, concurrently conclude the course and make a(nother) new beginning for a reading life beyond the delivered curriculum. In my delivered curriculum of the course, the graded activities were conventional: students had submitted

- Three essays, which were graded and "counted" for 15 percent each;
- A midterm (that sometimes is a midterm project) counting 15 percent;
- Class activities and homework counting 20 percent; and now
- The portfolio—which included one revised essay—that counted 20 percent, for a total of 100.

Accordingly, I asked students to create a portfolio that satisfied the following criteria:

The *literature portfolio* shows

- How you read
- How you have developed as a reader
- How you have developed as a reader of literature
- How you have developed as a writer about literature and literature-related topics/texts
- How you will continue to develop as a reader of many different kinds of texts

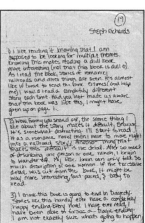

To show this development, students were asked to

- Include all three essays, one of which you have revised
- Include 3–7 other writings—including e-mails, in-class finger exercises, homework assignments, class projects—demonstrating the outcomes listed above

Informal questions about *The Octopus:*
What do you like about it?
What do you dislike?
How do you think the novel will end?

- Include one item that you shows you as a reader outside of class
- Include one reflective essay of 3–5 pages, in which you answer three of the five questions below:
  - ◆ As a reader of literature, what genres do you prefer, and why?
  - ◆ As a consumer of texts, how do you understand the relationship between literature and other kinds of texts?
  - ◆ What has been the most meaningful reading we have completed this term, and why?
  - ◆ How have you changed as a reader/writer this term?
  - ◆ Your choice.

This model of portfolio, like the model of English education portfolio and the model of writing portfolio that I prefer, is remarkable in three ways:

1. *It includes informal exhibits—homework assignments and in-class work—as well as formal assignments.* Through informal assignments, students often draw a conclusion, or make a connection, or try out an insight, or articulate a paradox, as we see here. Asked what she likes about reading *The Octopus*, Stephanie replies that she likes reading for multiple stories: "It's almost like if I were to read the book 5 times . . . I would read a completely different story each time." Asked what she *dislikes* about reading *The Octopus*, she says, "Wow, funny you should ask: the same thing I like about the story makes it difficult." These informal writings, then, show the "aha" moments of insight, connection, and thinking: the *palimpsest of learning*. Other times, of course, students in informal work begin to tease out an idea that leads to a defining question for them or to the question informing a formal assignment. In this case, we see the links between the informal and/leading to the formal.

Seen collectively and simultaneously, other informal pieces—like the reflection following a reader's theater performance and the print pop-up of a poem; the thinking about invisibility and the first rehearsals of what students don't understand; the maps of reading processes and the defining of pop-up contexts like epic and Western; and the questions about the poetry in "Stone Poem"—are the materials for another (invented) story, one that echoes the story told in the formal assignments, or one that runs counter to it. The archive of *these* pieces, then, holds the material traces of the student's learning. Including these pieces in the portfolio legitimates them, makes them count, and it asks the student to make connections between and among these pieces and between

Works and authors that students have read: *Maxim*, Thoreau, Ayn Rand, technical manuals, *Golf* magazine, Edna St. Vincent Millay, Edward Abbey, Henry Potter stories, *Glamour, Essence,* Web sites, *Lord of the Rings,* Robin Cook . . .

these and the more formal work. Equally important, the student chooses which of these to include, making judgments about which are important and why. In making these judg-

Table of Contents:

ments about what finally counts, the student has the responsibility and the opportunity to create the narrative of a reader.

2. *The student must include in the portfolio an exhibit from another setting.* If students bring into the class a lived curriculum, then they have been reading. The assumption is that they continue to read elsewhere, both in and out of school. Asking students to choose another text asks them to make that connection from this delivered curriculum to the lived curriculum by contextualizing it. In this way, a course portfolio has a programmatic aspect, located in the student's experience, given that she or he is making the choice, perceiving the connection, explaining its logic.

3. *Students engage in multiple kinds of revision.* Since

students are required to revise one of the three essays, they engage in (1) a *compositional revision;* since students may revise their midterm—and many do—they engage in (2) *a revision of a test;* since students are reviewing their own work, they may (3) *revise their understandings*—

> Narratives are not the distinguishing characteristic between a novel and a poem :)
>
> —Mandy

while at other times, there is no revision, although there is reflection—

> I must admit, I still do not get it when it comes to plays like <u>Waiting for Godot</u>. . . . However, I still believe that literature serves to connect people to each other, rather than to divide us into groups based on our preferences.
>
> —Lori

and at still other times, students find that they have (4) *revised their practices:*

> I have changed as a reader and writer this term but the changes are mainly in my interpretation of the works. It's kind of like I view literature in three dimensions now instead of two. I tend to give more thought to what the author was trying to say instead of accepting my first interpretation. I also pick up on important portions of literature more easily now, and think of the portions more as a whole and how they are related instead of having a bunch of independent facts going through my mind.
>
> —Dennis

In the fall of 2001, I decided to give students an option with portfolios: they could create print or digital portfolios. Five of the thirty-seven students in the class went electronic. I found that grading the portfolios in the digital format took less time; clicking can be fast. I also found that the criteria I used for the print portfolios—developing as a reader, developing as a reader of literature, and so forth—was necessary but insufficient. In particular, it failed to account for three factors specific to the digital:

1. How the student *links* across multiple (personal, contextual, academic) contexts
2. What kind of *interface* the student creates to connect various learnings/texts
3. How the student has used *design and technology*

Because this was a trial, the work of all students was governed by the old criteria, but as I read the five digital portfolios, I could see that the criteria needed to be changed to accommodate what the medium permits. I also found that going digital made sense given the kinds of activities characterizing the course, from mapping activities to PowerPoint presentations—indeed, from digitized essays (if they are created in a word-processing software, they are digitized) to listserv comments.

Not least, in this first iteration of a digital literature portfolio, I identified two items I hadn't seen in print. First, I found myself clicking outside of a student's work to link to work created by a team and then to link to work on the Web that provided context for the student work. In one portfolio, for instance, these links connected to a site on Edith Wharton and another on *House of Mirth*, both related to the student's work on invisibility in that novel. Second, the student connected—literally linked—her literature portfolio to a composition portfolio she had created the year before: she had carried forward a theme from that first portfolio:

One of the most important improvements that I have made this term is I have learned to express my thinking more clearly . The reflections that we write in class have helped with my thinking process. <u>I feel that expressing yourself clearly is the most important aspect of communication. John Henry Cardinal Newman put it well in "The Idea of a University."</u> <u>He stated, "It (college) is the education which gives a man a clear conscious view of his own opinions and judgments, a truth in developing them, an eloquence in expressing them, and a force in urging them."(page 89)</u> This first term, in college, I have learned about the importance in clearly expressing myself and its effects. [underlining mine]—Elizabeth Irwin

I have changed as a reader, writer and a thinker over this term. I have explained and illustrated what I have learned over the semester and how I have developed in different areas. I have also improved skills, learned new techniques and created my own way of interpretation. A tool that I will be sure to use in the future is using other text to understand literature and enjoy it, like popups. The reflections that we write in class have aided my thinking process. One of the most important improvements that I have made this term is making connections to my own experiences, which in turn has helped me to express thoughts more clearly. <u>I believe that clear expression of your ideas is the key to communication. John Henry Cardinal Newman put it well in "The Idea of a University." He stated, "It (college) is the education which gives a man a clear conscious view of his own opinions and judgments, a truth in developing them, an eloquence in expressing them, and a force in urging them"</u> (Page 89). I have come a long way over the past two years at Clemson in all areas of my study, but a continual goal for me as a writer and a thinker is to communicate effectively. I still have a lot to learn, but have taken yet one more step forward. [underlining mine] —Elizabeth Irwin

In print, no students, in my experience, had ever included such exhibits. In print, one *could* connect to outside sources of information, but students don't. (Neither do we: in reviewing teaching portfolios over the years, I've never seen a candidate link to a professional organization such as NCTE or MLA or CCCC, for example.) In print, one *can* carry forward themes—making them the temporal analogue to Booth's point about connecting learnings across sites—and we certainly hope that students do. Here, I literally *saw* the theme carried forward—and modified to accommodate the new course. Interestingly, because of that earlier portfolio, I was also able to see the student's work in a larger context. Her first reflective letter, for instance, was about 770 words, her letter this time over 1,500. I don't know that the second one is better, but I think it's more ambitious. She is developing over time, and she is attempting to make her progress meaningful in a coherent way. Also to the point, the student shows here the larger intellectual framework contextualizing her learning, a part of her *lived* curriculum. Had I known this as the term began, how might my knowledge have changed the course?

The next time I taught this course, I required all students to create a digital portfolio. For some students, this felt natural, but that didn't mean they were familiar with design or interface options. For other students, this was a frightening proposition; we met in a regular classroom (not a computer classroom), and they felt their skills weren't well enough developed, nor did they know design. On my campus, the skills issue is easy enough to address: we have an IT group that holds a workshop for classes on request, and a one-hour workshop in Netscape or Mozilla is adequate to the task, especially for a class that is not computer driven, much less computer informed. (In fact, both Microsoft Word and PowerPoint are sufficiently robust—with capacities for hyperlinking, audio, and video—for creating digital portfolios.) The design issue sounds easier to students (we all know what we like, after all) but isn't. While many students do use machines for much of daily life, from pushing a button on a VCR or DVD, to using e-mail and instant messaging, to ordering off the Web, most have not taken classes formally or otherwise in design. Moreover, as they begin to see what software permits—from animating bears to tie-dyeing the screen—it can be difficult to resist the many possibilities that technology enables. It's not about the technology, as I remind the students; it's about the medium. I did offer students models to show them what might be possible and to define this new genre for them, but in this first iteration, I did not "count" design (although that decision itself begs interesting questions about the relationship of form and content). I do now.

Ultimately, to a student, they liked creating digital portfolios. And as we shall see, what the digital allows students, as opposed to print, does vary. The situation is not either/or, but it is apples and oranges.

The reflective text is often considered the key item in any portfolio, and it's considered significant enough that some teachers assign it as a stand-alone assignment. In such a text (which can take several forms), the student both tells a story and raises questions, which, as Elinor Ochs and Lisa Capps suggest, are the two purposes of narrative:

> Developmental studies suggest, on the one hand, that as children grow older, their inclination to narrate habitual events is subsumed by the tendency to recount norm violations, and single utterances give way to temporally ordered, causally coherent narrative sequences. On the other hand, when children use narrative as a medium for making sense out of events, they are less willing to produce a linear account and more prone to doubts, questioning, and weighing alternative possible versions of an incident. (111)

Such is the case with reflective texts in this gen ed literature class. On the one hand, students do tend to tell their story of themselves intertwined with their story of the class. On the other hand, the story often takes not a linear path but a circuitous one, and one with conflicting impulses, as we see in Lori's observations:

> When I consider how I have developed as a reader, I think it is mainly that I have expressed in words that which I may already have known about reading, but have not actively discussed before. . . . As it turns out, the popularity of my favorite novels is probably due to their successful integration of multiple meanings. I do not know that I will continue to develop as a reader at this point in my life.

Here Lori charts her own development but does not know whether it will continue. She is content to read literature because she sees it as "connect[ing] people," and she does appreciate that she is "now more aware of different types of literature, and can now speak more generally and intelligently about literature." Earlier in her reflection, she demonstrated something about what that awareness looked like:

> I have learned a bit about relating literature to other texts and other forms of communication. One definition states that it must have multiple meanings in order to be good. Technical manuals,

the tools of my trade, are often referred to as literature, but by this definition they are not. The goal in technical writing is clarity, the less ambiguous the better. Therefore, one might say that technical manuals and textbooks are the opposite of literature. This would not be entirely correct, however, because they are both means of communication, therefore somehow connecting with others.

In this reflection, Lori performs both narrative tasks; she tells a story and she raises questions. She relates how the course played out for her; she can, as she says, talk about literature more "intelligently" now, and she has a finer sense of the similar dissimilarities (Booth) between and among the genres of technical manuals, textbooks, and literature. Put in terms of this project, she has delivered on the delivered curriculum. The experienced curriculum is that she now has a language for what she brought with her: "I have expressed in words that which I may already have known about reading, but have not actively discussed before," which in fact is what she brought with her—an appreciation of literature. Or: her lived curriculum. In other words, reflection offers the student an opportunity to plot the intersection of the three curricula.

We see a similar case with David:

1. *As a reader of literature, what genres do you prefer, and why?*

As a reader of literature, and when given the choice of what type of genres I prefer to read, I almost always lean toward novels. It isn't that I don't enjoy plays or poems, but rather that I would more enjoy a good novel when given the choice of the three genres stated above. Novels are filled with many characters, multiple stories, and rich in context, but these are only a few reasons as to why I enjoy reading novels. The best thing for me to do is to just give an example of what I believe is a "good" novel, and why.

> Here we see the language of the delivered curriculum: characters, multiple stories, rich context.

The Octopus, by Frank Norris, is a great example of a good novel. This novel has the ability to tell multiple stories at the same time. At one point in the novel you are reading about corruption, and at another point love. These are just two of the many stories that can be read in this novel. Of course, these stories are described in great detail. Novels are very rich in context,

> Here again we see the delivered curriculum.

which is another great attribute of novels. This context describes every detail of what a person looks like, what they are wearing, who they love, what their house looks like, and in general their every reason for living. At some points I find myself with a mental picture of all this because of the in depth detail that is given in novels. Another great attribute of a novel is its ability to make the reader feel. Being able to relate to and feel the emotion of what is being wrote about brings a novel to life. In a way, a novel can become a movie that plays in the readers head, giving the reader the ability to cast the characters, develop the setting, and give life to what

> David talks in terms of the *delivered* curriculum, using the language of genre to express the *experienced* curriculum (the movie that plays in the reader's head, here sounding very like Peter Elbow talking about movies in the mind, although of course we didn't read Elbow in class).

is being wrote about. These are just a few reasons as to why I enjoy reading novels, as compared to other forms of literature. As you can see from what I have stated above, novels are an interesting and enjoyable form of literature that would leave an empty space in our world without being present.

2. *What has been the most meaningful reading we have completed this term, and why?*

In my opinion, the *most meaningful reading* we completed this term was Invisible Man by Ralph Ellison. This is not because I enjoyed the book in general, although I did, but because of *the issues it raised in my own personal life*. We as American citizens, and I definitely include myself in this statement as well, go about our everyday lives blocking our, or making invisible, what we find to be upsetting, questionable, and offensive.

> This is a *direct question* about the *experienced curriculum,* of course, although to answer it fully, David calls on the *delivered* and then on the *lived* as well.

It seems to me that by doing this, we seem to believe that this makes it all go away. Because of this book and the presentations my English 202 class produced in conjunction with it, I have seen that out of sight does not always mean out of mind.

In my paper on invisibility, I answered the question: what is the role of invisibility in American culture? I answered this question by linking invisibility to the novel Invisible Man and the issue of homelessness in America. The homeless people are not by themselves when it comes to the issue of invisibility though. They are also joined by veterans, people who are over and underweight, the issue of racial inequality, homosexuality, and the list goes on and on. I came to the realization that I too made these issues and peoples stated above invisible. But the main reason why this reading was the most meaningful to me was because I too knew what it felt like to be invisible, yet in my everyday life, I never realized that I too was making others feel the same way that I did not want to feel. How could I ask to not be invisible in the way people viewed my weight (underweight), and turn around to not even acknowledge the way others were feeling, thus making them invisible. The answer to this problem of invisibility is as simple as this, do unto others as you would have them do unto you. [emphasis mine]

> Unlike David, I'm not sure the answer is as simple as this; clearly there are structural issues as well. But the delivered curriculum has linked to the experienced curriculum; David sees that, like all of us, he too is complicitous.

3. *How have you changed as a reader/writer this term?*

I can definitely say that I have changed as a reader and a writer this term. I have finished this course with the ability to read many different types of text, as well as write and talk about them. I can now read texts differently and thus understand them fully. This is a very important task if one wishes to write about the subject they have read. I also have the ability to write about what I have read in different forms. I have presented, this term, material in an essay format as well as an oral format. Both of

> Here David links the consumption of forms/genres with his own production of them and sees them as useful for his lived curriculum outside the class.

these formats will be very important as I continue my major of Business Marketing and in the career I develop from this major.

As I stated above, there are different forms in which to present what you have read. There are also different forms of literature, and I now know the importance of form in what I read. Knowing the different forms of literature, that is, whether something is a novel, a play, or a poem, has a lot to do with how you read. A good example of this is poetry.

> Here David concludes with a central issue in the delivered curriculum: How does/Does genre matter in text?

Before this term, I was scared to even think about poetry, much less read and interpret it. I now understand the importance of first finding the "plot" and then interpreting the poem. This course has helped mature me academically as well as personally. I now have the ability to read, write, and talk about literature more intellectually, which is something that I will appreciate every day of my life.

As I think about these portfolios, the familiar model of print and the newer Web-sensible digital, I understand that they are different in kind rather than degree and that their differences speak to the possibilities for student invention and representation.[1]

As Jay David Bolter and Richard Grusin explain in *Remediation: Understanding New Media*, and as Marshall McLuhan suggested even earlier, nearly every medium is re/mediated on another medium. In other words, consciously or otherwise, we create the new in the context of the old and based on the model of the old. Television is commonly understood to be remediated on film, for example, and the Web is commonly understood to be remediated on magazines. Remediation can be back-ended as well, as we see in the most recent CNN interface on television, which is quite explicitly remediated on the Web. As Bolter and Grusin observe, "Whenever one medium seems to have convinced viewers of its immediacy, other media try to appropriate that convention" (9). The new, then, repeats what came before, while at the same time remaking that which it models.

> Each of his films uses archetypal myths to underlie their plots, from the David and Goliath story of *Strictly Ballroom* to the Orpheus tale in *Moulin Rouge*. Luhrman also delights in hearing Shakespeare's Elizabethan English spoken by the gangbangers and new anchors in his *Romeo + Juliet*, or putting current American pop songs in the 1900 Paris of *Moulin Rouge*. He calls such devices "red curtain" gestures, overt theatrical stylizations that remind the audience they are not seeing "the naturalistic world," but a dramatic ritual that reenacts ancient universal myths.
> —Dana Gioia, "Moulin Rogue"

The idea that we refashion what came before is not, of course, limited to technology. Both W. Jackson Bate, in *The Burden of the Past and the English Poet*, and Harold Bloom, in *The Anxiety of Influence*, to cite two well-known examples, trace the influence of earlier canonical poets on later ones. The MoMA exhibit on Picasso and Matisse as well as recent scholarship exploring the relationship of John Quincy Adams to Thomas Jefferson make the same point about visual artists and the intellectual in public life, respectively. Within the world of film, we see this in many releases, such as *Moulin Rouge*, in which several rock songs are remediated. Interestingly, as is the case with technology, when the figures are contemporaneous—as with Wordsworth and Coleridge, Adams and Jefferson, and Matisse and Picasso—this influence often back-ends as well, so the relationship is more in the nature of a dialogue than of patriarchal influence.

Portfolios are likewise exercises in remediation. Like new media themselves, portfolios "emerge from within cultural contexts, and they re-fashion other media, which are embedded in the same or similar contexts " (Bolter and Grusin, 19). From this perspective, a print portfolio seems remediated on a book. Typically, it opens with a letter or table of contents and then proceeds in a linear fashion from beginning to end. It privileges a single story, typically an argument or a narrative that argues; it highlights the story of development told by the writer; and it culminates in a narrative of accomplishment. Like chapters in a book, the entries in the portfolio

> We have been made to see more clearly the assumptions that come with a book: it is authoritative and unchangeable, transparent and unselfconscious, read in silence and, if possible, in private.
> —Richard Lanham

This portfolio has been composed into the form of a book with chapters. I believe this is an interesting and organized way to follow the different sorts of genres worked on in class throughout the semester. The essays make up the first chapter. They are put in chronological order followed by the revised edition. Chapter two is an assorted mixture of two different genres: poetry and my thoughts written in class. These two are alike because they have meaning, and the ideas are condensed. However, they are different because the poems are real literature while the ideas reflect back onto the poems and other things we have done in class. The readings from outside of class are put in the third chapter because they are provided by the news and entertainment media not from the classroom. I put the reflective essay in the very last chapter because as the components of this portfolio reflect what has been done throughout the semester, the essay will do that as well. Finally the appendix as an added section full of rough drafts of the essays in chapter one. [boldface mine]
—Mandy

testify to this story line. Although the reader may move through the portfolio hypertextually—and, as Jeff Sommers has suggested, portfolio readers often do (Allen et al.)—the linear arrangement of the book argues for a beginning-to-end reading. The reader of the portfolio is, more often than not, singular: the teacher. The portfolio is typically read in isolation, silently. Because of the print medium, which outside of a school culture culminates in a publication that is revised only if the number of copies sold is sufficient, the argument is frozen in a particular point in time: a print portfolio is, typically, published only once. And once published, the story opens, progresses, and, most important, concludes. In sum, the arrangement of the portfolio, modeled on a book, provides for the invention of a particular kind of student: one who can state a claim, synthesize material, lead a reader through a tale of progress and achievement, and conclude.

Still, a print portfolio *is* a remediation: as such, it offers more and other than a conventional book. A book, for instance, is the product of many processes, most of which are invisible: what we tend to see in the finished product is the trace of the processes that produced it. In contrast, a print portfolio, particularly a classroom print portfolio and especially one including process as well as informal exhibits, does intend to show process—it proposes to show the ropes and pulleys that went into the final publication as well as the final publication itself. Much like Coosje van Bruggen's *Frank O. Gehry: Guggenheim Museum Bilbao*, which records in reiterative detail the museum's "conception through design and construction," a print portfolio shows us the *how* of development as well as the achievements *of* it. In the terms of literary theorist Michael Davidson, what a print portfolio offers, in this way of process and product, is a palimtext, "the still-visible record of its responses to earlier writings" (78). Palimtext here is a participle: it intends to show the "making" of writing, the making of knowledge, the making of understanding, and perhaps the making of wisdom—all of which a student may elect to show in the portfolio.

As students compose the print portfolio, showing both the making and the made, they engage in activities that the authors of *The Myth of the Paperless Office* identify as knowledge making. The product of research into the activities of "knowledge workers," *The Myth of the Paperless Office* outlines the myriad processes of the gathering, storing, and sorting of documents that writers use to "construct and organize thoughts" (Sellen and Harper, 61), processes that, the authors claim, rely quite explicitly on the presence and arrangement of print documents. Writers, for example, keep information available as "contextual cues to remind them of where they were in *the space of ideas*" (61; italics mine). The "laying out of the paper reports" and the "time bringing together and organizing reports for themselves or other people" are two critical activities for making knowledge. Another is the

> act of flicking through these documents, bringing to mind what was important to them and why they were important. The main implication of all this is that paper is important because it makes information accessible and tangible and gives it a persistent presence. (63)

The collection and arrangement of documents, as with portfolios, permit the creation of knowledge needed in an information age. And the pattern, Sellen and Harper claim, is consistent across a diversity of workplaces:

> Since the time of our study, we have noticed that when we look at most workplaces, it is easy to see who is engaged in intensive knowledge work: it is the person whose desk is strewn with paper. Find a desk littered with stacks of reports, written notes, and every inch of space used up, and you will find someone creating a document, planning work, or doing some other sort of deeply reflective activity. (72)

As we have seen, portfolios are exercises in *deeply reflective activity*. More generally, print portfolios, by virtue of the medium, ask students to engage in processes leading to knowledge and processes associated with reflective thinking.

Not least, the coherence achieved in the print portfolio is a verbal coherence, as is the means of representation. Put in terms of Howard Gardner's multiple intelligences, print portfolios are more singular than plural.

Digital portfolios, like their print cousins, are exercises in remediation. They can remediate in one of two ways. Some electronic portfolios, even though they are created in a digital environment, remediate a print model. This portfolio is the academic analogue to the print catalog: a genre that is written for the page, not the screen, and whose digitality serves one of two single purposes: easier storage or quicker dissemination. As I have said elsewhere, it is one version of print uploaded (Wickliff and Yancey). Its arrangement is identical to that of a print model: regardless of the fact that it is housed in the digital environment, it does not participate in the environment, and the student resembles her print cousin—she is the invention of print.

> Whatever else learning may be, it is clearly *a disposition to form structures.*—Ann Berthoff (in Tinburg)

But other digital portfolios enact another remediation, this one less print portfolio than digital gallery. Like a gallery, a digital portfolio has a central entry point, which for portfolios is typically called a portal. Like a gallery, the digital portfolio includes both text and image, using the one modality to explain and juxtapose the other. Like a gallery, the digital portfolio makes multiple contexts a part of the display, which means linking internally to the student's own work and linking externally to multiple worlds outside the student's purview to show

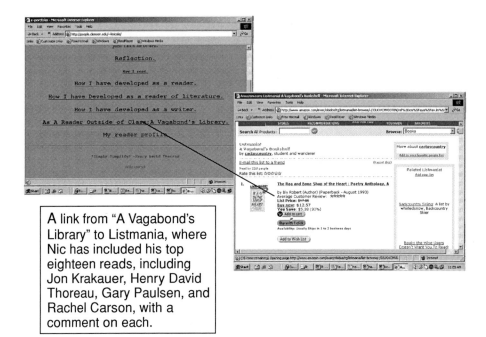

A link from "A Vagabond's Library" to Listmania, where Nic has included his top eighteen reads, including Jon Krakauer, Henry David Thoreau, Gary Paulsen, and Rachel Carson, with a comment on each.

multiple and complex relationships. The readership for a digital portfolio is likewise multiple, as are the ways of processing the portfolio; often, there is an implied linear path, but that may be interrupted by peripheral links that take the reader to the nooks and crannies of the digital portfolio gallery. In the language of linguistics, digital portfolios can right branch, and they right branch again; they left branch, and they left branch again. Cumulatively and literally, the right and left branches produce a layered literacy that is different in kind from the thesis-and-support literacy of the print model. Depth of thought is created and demonstrated through multiple contexts: evoked verbally, evoked visually, evoked through internal links, evoked through external links. The arrangement of this portfolio, modeled on the gallery, thus provides for the invention of a particular kind of

Print text at least gives the author the opportunity to suggest a default path through the text. The author can also assume, or write as if she assumes, that the average reader will read the entire text. The author of hypertext can make no such assumption. The reader can find no default path, no suggested order of text blocks from one page to the next, and can never be sure that she has found every node. The constructedness of text, underground in print, is now in your face. Linking becomes not just possible, but easy, natural, inevitable. This is what pushes the text over the break boundary.—Brent student: one who can make multiple connections and who creates depth through multiplicity and elaboration, who can work in visual and verbal and aural modalities, who can offer a reader multiple narratives extending ever outward. This portfolio is the electronic text described by Richard Lanham in *The Electronic Word:* "No 'final cut' means no conventional endings or beginnings or middles either. Interactive literary texts will require some basic non-Aristotelian adjustments" (11).

If, then, the print portfolio is Aristotelian, the digital is post-Aristotelian. Equally important, the digital portfolio seems more like a gallery as students develop portfolios that span contexts, that link different kinds of experiences, and that project into the future after the course ends. Indeed, the digital portfolio, located in multiple and multiple kinds of relationships, is a *digital composition:* a single, unified text through which various fragments, both rational and intuitive, are related to each other, directly, associatively.

Because you can link externally as well as internally and
because those links are material,
you have more contexts you can link to,
more strata you can layer,
more you to invent,
more invention to represent.

In the context of a literature portfolio, what do students say they have learned? And what else might we all learn?

1. They like generalizing across texts and across media. They are accustomed to reading a specific poem, to finding its thesis, and to focusing there. They aren't used to finding multiple stories, to making the connections between here and the world. They like making these connections: sometimes the connections are there for the taking; sometimes students invent them. To cite one example, when thinking about invisibility in *The Invisible Man, The House of Mirth,* and *The Handmaid's Tale,* one group created a Web site making visible the people around us whom we tend to make invisible; another group looked at the role that invisibility played in the lives of Ralph Ellison, Langston Hughes, and Edith Wharton. (Does art imitate life?) In making the connections formally, students are often inventing new material; they are inventing themselves.

2. Students like the strategies we develop for reading, both the process representations, such as maps that allow them to ana-

lyze their own reading and thinking, and the sources, such as the *New York Times* Web, that can support their future reading.

3. A key here is networking: among associations, among authors, among genres, among groups of readers. How can we create and sustain these networks? What role should a gen ed literature course play in fostering such networking?

4. Students like thinking in terms of genre. Approached this way—what is poetic in a novel?—they find the concept flexible, rhetorical, and helpful, in terms of both reading and understanding what was read. They also can begin to see themselves as consumers of text and thus begin to develop a critical reading practice. To do that, the benefit from the distancing effect of narrative and reflection: they can look at themselves and at their own practice.

5. Students like reading for multiple stories, though not always for the reasons I intended. The *delivered* curriculum included multiple stories so students would read more flexibly and read as "other"; students *experience* a set of stories that enables them to organize their reading and sustain it. Through multiple stories, students find themselves actively constructing texts and interpeting them.

6. As students create new digital compositions, the interfaces might become more intentional, designed more to connect to the readings. Suppose, for instance, that the interface for a digital portfolio were modeled on a house, to mimic *The House of Mirth*. Which rooms would be created? Which rooms would house which exhibits and why? (What relationships would be created?) How might these 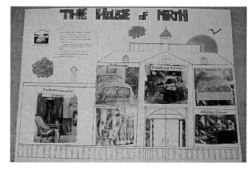 connect to *House of Mirth*? And what kind of learning would we see then?

7. Several questions have to do with the relationships between and among linking, learning, and connecting. Is there a relationship between electronic linking and cognitive linking? Does the kind of link matter?

8. Let's assume that the portfolios—print and digital—invite different representations and thus different inventions. If this is so, should we ask students to create two portfolios, perhaps one in print in the middle of the term and then another—digi-

tal—model at the end? What would students tell us they learn in each? How might those learnings connect?

9. What are the best reflective questions? Around this single question are clustered many others, including

- Are there questions that work well to link reading and writing, such as questions about genre?

- What about questions that link to literacy practices that usually happen outside of school, like video games and instant messaging?

- Are there questions that students should pursue for years rather than months? What would such a practice contribute to the coherence of a gen ed literature program?

- What would a content analysis of reflective texts tell us about the relationships between the lived, delivered, and experienced curricula?

Through portfolios, students create selves; the medium that we invite or require functions as an exigence, permitting certain responses, certain representations. Through portfolios, students can map the three curricula of any learning site: the lived, the delivered, and the experienced. Not least, through reading students' portfolios, we have a better understanding of our own teaching. We learn, too.

Note

1. Portions of the following discussion are adapted from Kathleen Blake Yancey's essay "Postmodernism, Palimpsest, and Portfolios: Theoretical Issues in the Representation of Student Work" published in *College Composition and Communication* 56.4 (2004): 738–61. Reprinted with permission.

6 Teaching Literature as Reflective Practice: A Reflective Conclusion

When the blackbird flew out of sight
It marked the edge
Of one of many circles

Wallace Stevens, "Thirteen Ways
of Looking at a Blackbird"

I want to begin the closing of this volume as I opened it, with five observations.

Observation One. We all read out of our own experience, both literally and metaphorically (as we have seen). When I began teaching literature for general education students, I looked for some guidance. The catalog copy, a local source, provided parameters but no particular outcomes or goals connected to general education. When I looked across the country, I didn't find the help I was seeking—which means that I'm on my own. I can teach literature out of one tradition, say American naturalism. I can teach a version of world lit. I can thematize it, as one colleague did, into a course on apocalyptic visions. I can move chronologically in a history-of-literature mode. I can include electronic poetry, hypertext novels, and/or film. I can do some mix of any of the above.

If you like academic freedom, and I do, *any mix of the above* may sound ideal. *Not quite*, I'd say. To paraphrase, no teacher is an island,[1] which for me means that I want to think about this course's context as *occurring within* a specific context and *participating in* that context (Bakhtin); and thus I want to think about it as a specific *kind* of course, what we might call the *genre of a course.* For nearly every course I teach—from rhetoric, to professional communication, to English methods, to first-year composition, and now to "Studio Composition and Communication"—I have a "given" context, what we might think of as a rhetorical situation doubled: the local rhetorical situation *and* a national context. The *course as genre* is a response to both. What I wanted for this course was a larger rhetorical situation in which to situate it.

Observation Two. We *do* read out of our own experience. A former neighbor, a college graduate from a "good" university, works hard, loves his children, volunteers for the community, commands a greater salary than I ever will, and, as far as I can tell, pays his bills on time. He does not read. It's not that he doesn't read literature: it's that he does not *read*. When I teach the general education literature course, I see his younger self in my class.

Observation Three. I don't know exactly what it is we want general education to do; that, it seems to me, is a question no single faculty member could answer. At the same time, I do have a philosophy of general education, the features of which include intellectual play and multiplicity of several kinds, the aims of which have something to do with democracy, with informed citizens, with reflective human beings. As we have seen, current talk about general education—Scholes's ("Transition") connection of the class text with the world text, for example, and McGann et al.'s interest in reflection, and, before them, Rosenblatt's aims of reading and Dewey's interest in experience—is congruent with like changes in the academy. As Cantor and Schomberg claim,

> In a sense, universities, like theaters in which performers play with reality, are proving grounds as well as training grounds for society. We are set apart from, yet remain closely tethered to, the real worlds from which our students come and to which they will return. This distanced, yet engaged, positioning of universities situates us as places of transformation for our students (and for ourselves). (n. pag.)

This connection—between the academy and the world—seems to be one of the distinguishing attributes of current models of education; we see it expressed in service learning, in internships, in volunteer service, in travel abroad programs. In this model of education, university service takes on a new meaning, and general education is a keystone of that effort.

If this description and analysis are accurate, it's still fair to ask, why literature? What is it about literary study that makes it a worthy ground for intellectual play and for democratic values? In other words, a number of disciplines might help students become more reflective and informed citizens, more aware of and appreciative of democracy and diversity. Rhetoric comes to mind, as does philosophy and political science and . . . Why literature? Like the question about general education, this isn't one I can answer by myself. But I do have an answer for myself, even though it may be self-evident: I think that reading literature can make one a better reader (1) given the multiple layers within a literary text and thus the many opportunities and ways of making meaning provided by that text; (2) given how any genre influences what we read—as David says, "Knowing the different forms of literature, that is, whether something is a novel, a play, or a poem, has a lot to do with how you read"—; and (3) given the issues that literature, which isn't real, (ironically) makes more real than reality. I also think that working through literary texts can make one think, not only individually, but also communally; we see this in Oprah's book parties, in poetry jams, in book clubs that are a staple of life for women particularly, even

> Humanities has made itself irrelevant by not taking undergraduate education seriously. By not considering the classroom as 'our laboratory.' By not healing the rift b/w [1]. k-12 and Higher Ed [2]. the technological gap b/w rich and poor [3]. inner life (the creative/analytic mind) and the public good (applied knowledge).
> —Chidsey Dickson, "Summary"

if much of the United States is *Bowling Alone* (Robert Putnam). Communality is fundamental. We are different; we do bring different values to bear, even as we learn from and with others. In the final analysis, conflict and war are rooted in values. Reading together, allowing others to read a text differently than we do, and respecting that difference, even learning from it; learning to talk about texts and (their) issues in a reflective way; learning to see issues though another eye: it's the best hope for a world without war, the best hope for a democracy in which "talking back," in bell hooks's language, is *normal*. Literature can provide a mechanism for doing all this in a general education program suited to these aims.

Observation Four. Elizabeth Daley, dean of the University of Southern California's School of Cinema-Television and executive director of its Annenberg Center, argues in "Expanding the Concept of Literacy" that new media are rewriting our conceptions of literacy, and contends that "those who are truly literate in the twenty-first century will be those who learn to both read and write the multimedia language of the screen" (34). Interestingly, she notes that media study, *a reading of the screen* intended to develop the critical acumen of a consumer (but not to develop her or his design of such communications), *is* part of the high school English curriculum. She specifically mentions the role that the National Council of Teachers of English has played in this curriculum. But something happens in that transition to college, she (rightly) says: media study gets lost. Daley believes that media literacy, both consumption and creation, is the *new* literacy, although she doesn't look to English to provide it. She argues that

> students will need to be taught to read and write cinematic language, the language you and I speak, the language of the screen, of sound and image, just as they are now taught to read and write print. . . . Otherwise, won't they be just as illiterate as you or I would have been upon leaving college if we were unable to write the proverbial essay? ("Screen as Vernacular," n. pag.)

Comparing the current situation to that of scholars at the University of Padua whose teaching in Latin changed once Italian came "inside" the academy, Daley suggests that the current situation is parallel. Faculty inside today's academy will have to change their concept and practices of literacy given pressures from the outside that, she says, already infuse the vernacular:

> Metaphors from the screen have become common in our daily conversation. If you think about it for a moment, we use "close-up" as synonymous for in-depth and penetrating because we believe it reveals through magnification. We speak of "flashing back" to our earlier lives; we "frame" events to put them into context; we "cut to the chase"; we "dissolve" or "fade-out" or "segue" from one topic to another; we worry about "background noise." We spend hours at our computers "sharing screens." ("Screen as Vernacular," n. pag.)

Daley also argues if we make this change to a multiple literacy, we will make learning available to all students in ways that, given the ascendance of print, we have not previously. This, she promises, will democratize education.

Observation Five. I've thought for some time that the model of education we tend to favor is what I'd call the FedEx truck model of curriculum. We package curriculum, load it into the FedEx truck, and send it on its way to our students. We assume that the curriculum is delivered to the student's door; through our lectures and assignments, we certainly delivered it. Still, we check our assumption by testing the student on the contents of the truck, checking also that the delivery arrived exactly on (our) time. We don't ask what else might have been delivered, or what the student might want to send back to us, or whether the student is even at home to accept delivery or what that home looks like.

If we changed our model of curriculum, and if we changed the questions we asked, and if we changed when we asked them—for instance, asking students what they don't know at the *beginning* of the term rather than at the end—we might find that this truck wasn't the right vehicle with which to deliver curriculum after all.

I've long been interested in the relationship between curriculum and its delivery. In teaching eighth graders in rural Maryland some twenty-five years ago, I saw immediately that "my" delivery, designed for seventeen-year-old suburban, college-prep students, was failing. (When an approach fails in class, we don't really need anyone to tell us; students do that all too well.) Quickly, I abandoned the textbooks the students couldn't read and the circled chairs where students were to discuss the stories (they could not read). Eventually, the chairs were returned to a circle and stories were discussed, but not until I had designed a curriculum for *those* students.

Some fifteen years later, in reviewing students' portfolios, especially in English education classes, I came to understand that what I think I deliver *isn't delivered but rather constructed*—differently from one student to the next. What I had sensed intuitively—that there was an *experienced* curriculum—was documented in the portfolios. I began to understand curriculum as multiple.

In other classes I was teaching at the same time, I was developing appropriate uses of technology for my classes. In talking about such adaptations with colleagues inside my department and across campus, I've seen how the medium alters what we deliver, raising curricular and pedagogical questions about the relationship of medium/form and content, the very questions I often find animating my literature classes.[2] Many of the students in those technologically enhanced classes brought with them an expertise they had developed outside of school, their *lived* curriculum. And just as my students' reflections had enhanced their thinking, much of my thinking, especially about this topic, was informed and enhanced by those same reflections, both informal and formal, that students had shared. I began to see the curriculum as plural: the delivered curriculum I might design; the experienced curriculum students would construct; the lived curriculum that contextualized both.

Reflection—which we currently see in Stephen Brookfield's work on teaching, in George Hillocks's work on teaching writing, in my own work on teaching writing and on portfolios, in Jerome McGann et al.'s recent work on the teaching of literature—holds out the hope that students can be engaged, can map their own learning, can make their own knowledge, *with us*. In other words, reflection—both formal and informal, used to review texts and experience and to think about what learnings might be plotted in the future—promises to change the school game, in part because it encourages a kind of expectation of success. As June Birnbaum explains,

> Although the widespread characterization of better readers and writers as reflective thinkers is a relatively recent one, the importance of reflective thought in problem solving has long been a major theme in the psychological literature. In 1963, J. Kagan, B. L. Rosman, D. Day, J. Albert, and W. Phillips, seeking to explain differences in cognitive styles, or ways of perceiving and processing experiences, found underlying differences among the conceptual tempos of their subjects. They termed these differences the "reflective-impulsive dimension." According to these investigators, reflectiveness is rooted in expectation of mastery rather than anxiety about failure. Reflective thinkers tend to pause and deliberate over alternative solutions to problems when these are simultaneously available and to inhibit incorrect hypotheses before reporting public solutions. In contrast, the impulsives' anxiety over failure leads them to seize the first possible solution to a problem and give it public report. Thus reflectives seem able to exert a control over their cognitive processes that impulsives seem to lack. (32)

This control, of course, is acquired. In a classroom setting, particularly a classroom setting where literature is the focus, where collaborative learning is common, and where performance is a part of the delivered curriculum, reflection is concurrently an individual and a social opportunity to *pause*, to *deliberate*, to consider and to *embody alternatives*, and to articulate the curricula and the learning within and across them.

It's an interesting question, what the general education literature course of the future is going to look like. I don't think that offering students only what they have studied before—either what they have already studied in high school or what and how they studied in the last century—will be

> Nineteenth century images of classrooms with the instructor standing on a raised dais over students seated in desks bolted to the floor, of teachers caning students' bodies, and of students standing to recite have given way to the more familiar images of instructors seated near students, of moveable desks arranged in a semi-circle, and of students' fingers poised over a keyboard.—Anne Ruggles Gere

very successful. Even if students haven't been back to the future, they think they have. Given the ubiquity of textual practices of all kinds—from handheld text messaging devices, to video games, to online newspapers (like *The Onion*, issues of which, in a classic case of remediation, have been collected in a multivolume print publication), to user manuals and, yes, even magazines and books—students come to class with their own sense of genre and media, part of their *lived* curriculum. In general, this lived curriculum differs from that of most teachers, even now. (When I say to colleagues that we will never know as much technology as our students, everyone laughs, not quite apologetically. No one tries to resist.)[3]

At the same time, students' interest in taking up big questions that focus on literature itself, that link life to literature, and that rely on literature as a means of thinking philosophically and reflectively has not changed. This continuing interest provides another way to think about the general education literature course: we might ask, what kind of conversation will such a course promote? In considering and reflecting on this question, I've identified three prototype claims I offer here as exemplars. Each of them outlines an interesting claim, in the process raising good, not-quite-answerable questions, questions located in literature but not confined to it, the kinds of questions that could point us toward a literature course designed explicitly for general education. Each claim is rooted in a vocabulary, a frame of reference; each invites reading experience, careful observation, and reflective judgment. Relying on contrast to differentiate, each concurrently invites synthesis.

The first claim comes from the *Washington Post* in a review by Jonathan Yardley, in which he theorizes about the United States and our literature. Focusing specifically on the novel, Yardley begins by noting how the United States is different from other countries in its dearth of enthusiasm for a "serious" literature. From the beginning, he says,

> almost all of our writers have been on the margin—even the insiders, notably Edith Wharton and John P. Marquand, really are outsiders—doing work that interests few Americans and that even fewer understand or appreciate. Writing serious literature here has always been a struggle, for the obvious reason that its economic rewards are proportionately as small as the readership it attracts, but also for the more complicated one that the American writer is outside the mainstream and therefore is inclined to be skeptical about, if not outright hostile to, conventional society, its habits and mores and institutions.

Is this assertion true? In some novels (e.g., *The Scarlet Letter*), yes, it seems to be. Is it so in others, say *The Great Gatsby* or *Winesburg, Ohio*? Is this a defining tension in our literature? If so, what does it say about us? Where is it not true, and why not? And what of *other* literatures? And/or is this really a statement about the relationship of the artist to society? How does the poet laureate fit into this understanding? The public intellectual, such as Henry Louis Gates Jr.? (Is this what we see in current literature?) What is the appropriate relationship?

The second claim is grounded in a *New Yorker* article profiling Toni Morrison as person, editor, and writer:

> Situating herself inside the black world, Morrison undermined the myth of black cohesiveness. With whiteness offstage, or certainly right of center, she showed black people fighting with each other—murdering, raping. . . . She also showed nurturing fathers who abide and the matriarchs who love them. Morrison reveled in the complications. "I didn't want it to be a teaching tool for white people. I wanted it to be true—not from outside the culture, as a writer looking back at it," she said. "I wanted it to come from inside the culture, and speak to people inside the culture. . . ." Doing so, Morrison broke ranks—particularly with black male writers such as Larry Neal and Amiri Baraka. . . . Their attitude descended from the realistic portraits of black resistance in the novels of Wright, Baldwin, and Ellison—who, Morrison believed, were writing for a white audience. "The title of Ralph Ellison's book was 'Invisible Man,'" Morrison said. "And the question for me was 'Invisible to whom?' Not to me." (Als)

Here is another way to think about literature: as working within specific discourse communities such as African American, Latino American, Chinese American. What is the relationship between each smaller culture and the larger culture? Within each culture, is there a kind of movement, as suggested by Morrison, with writing from the *outside* for a larger (white) public preceding writing from the *inside* for those within the culture? What difference does it make? What would this understanding of literature tell us about ourselves? Is the claim about *Invisible Man* accurate? My students, most of whom are white, like *Invisible Man*— and so do the African American and Indian American and Korean American students. Regardless of whether Ellison had those students in mind, he succeeds with them. To employ the metaphor of the novel, they seem to see differently. As noted earlier, they also tend to universalize it, seeing invisibility as something that crosses cultures. To be fair, in some measure they see the novel this way because of the way I set it up. To counter this tendency (and does it need to be countered?), might we pair it with a novel such as *Sula* or *Beloved*, and might we use this sequence and set of questions as a context? (If we were to take this approach, and include this pairing as the delivered curriculum, what would students experience? Would they forgo voluntarily linking Ellison and Langston Hughes, or *Invisible Man* and *House of Mirth*? Or suppose we linked Ellison and Drabble? What is the value of *these* pairings?)

The third exemplar also comes from the *New Yorker,* this time a review of the movie *In the Cut* by David Denby:

> The movie [an adaptation of the novel of the same name] has been entirely pre-arranged for dreadfulness. This isn't true of Susanna Moore's novel. Working in a neo-hardboiled style that she fine-tuned into elegance, Moore created a cool and dry first-person voice for Frannie. . . . Moore worked with Campion on the screenplay, so presumably Frannie turned out the way she wanted, but she may not have realized how much of her compositional poise would be lost when that voice got transformed into overwrought camera rhetoric, a distorted color scheme, and the flounderings of a charming but inadequate actress. (112)

This conversation, taking up issues of what happens to text when it moves from one medium to another, speaks to "literary" issues: character, composition, literature, voice. Likewise, it speaks to the role of the author, the role of the director, and the ways that each makes character known—and the role that we as readers/viewers play in that process, how we become co-composers. This conversation isn't about using film to enhance the literature, but rather about different media presenting what is ostensibly the same story in different venues. Within that claim lie fundamental questions: Is it the *same* story? If so, which is "better" and why? Does that matter? What do we learn from each? How does each delight? Not least, is Yusef Komunyakaa correct when he says, "I believe content is a part of process, which is essential to technique and form"? This last question itself is sufficiently capacious to ground a course in general education literature. Teasing out what such a claim means, within the context of both consumption and creation, might help students negotiate all three curricula.

If we read across the three examples, the questions speak to big-picture issues: the Americanness of literature and the role it plays in speaking to and representing a diversity of experiences; the relationship of artist to public, of public to literature; the ways that texts read when they are placed in different contexts; the role of form and content as art transverses media. When students read for the big picture, when they speak to questions such as these through the specifics of particular texts, they create contexts that invite new readings, during the course and after.

This, it seems to me, is a primary purpose of a general education literature course.

> I know noble accents
> And lucid, inescapable rhythms;
> But I know, too,
> That the blackbird is involved
> In what I know.
>
> Wallace Stevens, "Thirteen Ways
> of Looking at a Blackbird"

My work on this project, grounded in my sense of general education and of the lived curriculum taking place twenty-four hours a day, leads me to draw four conclusions:

1. The teaching of literature needs to be, first, a course in reading.

2. When we teach literature, we need to include the joy of literature.

3. If students are going to be readers of literature, they will have to learn the "how" of reading.

4. Literature is published in multiple media; our courses in literature need to be equally inclusive.

Let me explain.

The teaching of literature needs to be, first, a course in reading. John Guillory makes the point that the teaching of literature as the teaching of reading is not a new idea, that the New Critics were reading teachers themselves and their scholarship principally a scholarship of reading. In our affection for theory, Guillory says, reading got lost. That's part of it, no doubt, but another is that most teachers of high school and college don't identify as reading teachers:

> Reading is not something that one learns to do once in elementary school; it is a lifelong process of growth as one meets the challenges of new texts. When we signed on to be English teachers, many of us thought that "teaching reading" was something that someone else did. (Christenbury)

As it turns out, reading is a process that extends well into high school and college; it might be, in fact, like writing, a process benefiting from lifelong study, lifelong practice. Students like and

> I'm in a state of perpetual reader's block. . . . I can barely finish one book per month and the only reason I finish the *one* is because I don't want to miss book club. Case in point. . . . I knew I was going to miss book club this month so I never even picked up *Watership Down*. I have been reading *Harry Potter and the Order of the Phoenix* and am about to start next month's selection. Reader's block is a fact of life for me. . . . I just don't have the time to read during the school year.[4]—Jdroth

benefit from reflecting on their own reading; reader's block, through the analysis of a reading map, can be broken. We might also think about what kinds of reading we might bring into a general education literature course, perhaps nonfiction as well as fiction and poetry and drama, perhaps attention to reading practices in other disciplines. As David Schwalm suggests, without such attention, and given the current culture, the very nature of literature is at risk:

> As readers, students recognize that they have to pay attention to what is said in their textbooks because it's "true." The front page of the paper is "true" too. The instructions for downloading mp3s are true too. The editorial page is opinion. And with "literature"? Heck, relax. You've got to learn the names of the characters and stuff so you can score well on the identification parts of the tests. But the rest? Breeze through it once, figure it's about sex or death, and go to work at Walmart.

When we teach literature, we need to include the joy of literature. As Louise Rosenblatt has explained, literature brings with it a pleasure derived from the aesthetic. Finding a way to help students experience this joy is one task of the delivered curriculum. This project attests to the joy in literature that students find when they *participate in the literature*—by means of performing reader's theater, or finding poetry in a sculpture, or performing a pop-up. bell hooks explains why such participation is so important:

> Poetry came into my life, the sense of poetry, with reading scripture with those awkward and funny little rhymes we would memorize and recite on Easter Sunday. Then it came into my life at Booker T. Washington grade school where I learned that poetry was no silent subject. The moment of learning was pure enchantment, for we learned by listening and reciting that words put together just so, said just so, could have the same impact on our psyches as song, could lift and exalt our spirits, enabling us to feel tremendous joy, or carrying us down into that most immediate and violent sense of loss and grief. (10)

Poetry, hooks says, is "no silent subject": it is "memorize[d] and recite[d]," "listen[ed]" to, "exalt[ing]."

If students are going to be readers of literature, they will have to learn the "how" of reading, a claim that is more complex than it sounds. For one thing, students need to understand something about how literature works, and as reviewer Michael Dirda explains, the literary world, and the logic underlying it, can be difficult to make out:

> Literature isn't just fun and games, but literary reputation can sometimes seem little more than that. One day you're the most

highly regarded, critically acclaimed, bestselling novelist of the 1920s, and the next you're "Joseph Hergesheimer, who he?" Twenty-five years ago, Zora Neale Hurston was a half-forgotten African-American writer; now she's in the Library of America, and her books are taught in high schools and colleges even more than those of Toni Morrison. Who's up, who's down, who's the champ, and who's the chump—it can all seem like a bizarre, slightly unreal game.

One issue, then, is *demystifying the culture of literature* and helping students understand how it works and thus how trends like these occur. Another issue is to use not-understanding and exploration rather than argument and certainty as principal intellectual moves. Yet another issue is one that I think we as teachers need to reconcile: how do we work with a text to make meaning, and how much interpretive license do we have? When the New Critics held sway, no context was required at all. Some two decades later, context was everything; no poem could be read without the accompanying gloss, and this was particularly true for "newer" literatures like Native American. Admittedly, some of the images and symbols in some of the new literature were unfamiliar to many, but that was part of their charm. When

> While the aristocratic Henry James retreated to England, which he found more congenial than his native land, Edith Wharton made Manhattan society into the raw material for novels—most notable *The House of Mirth* and *The Age of Innocence*—in which it was proved conclusively that *the manners of society at any level contain stories about society as a whole*. [italics mine]
> —Yardley

students leave our classes to join the community of the reading public, do we expect that before reading a new literature or a new author they will do background reading first? If they don't, how do they acquire the context we provide in class and that so many of us think is important? Is this our practice? Or is the background reading sometimes motivated by the new literature? In other words, how universal is literature? Do we think it is acceptable for people to read without our guidance? If we want an informed and reflective reading public, I don't see how it can be any other way, and these are the practices that we need to help students learn. And if literacy is dialogic, even multilogic, then we will learn as well.

A related question: how personally and universally do we want students to read themselves into the text? Cynthia Ozick points out in "Who Owns Anne Frank?" that even good motives can be thwarted, and they can be thwarted particularly when we reduce the individual to a type, when we, like the characters in Carson McCullers's *The Heart Is a*

Lonely Hunter, project our (universal) needs onto that figure. Ozick makes this point by citing correspondence between an American student, Cara Wilson (née Weiss), and Otto Frank, Anne's father. Wilson's identification with Anne derives from her reading of Anne's diary, and, as she makes clear, such a reading is permeated (indeed determined) by the tropes of affluent American youth:

> I was miserable being me. . . . I was on the brink of that awful abyss of teenagedom and I, too, needed someone to talk to. . . . Dad's whole life was a series of meetings. At home, he was too tired or frustrated to unload on. I had something else in common with Anne. We both had to share with sisters who were smarter and prettier than we were. . . . (qtd. in Ozick, 79)

Ozick's objection to such reader projection onto the diary stems primarily from her sense of how it dilutes history: "any projection of Anne Frank as a contemporary figure is an unholy speculation: it tampers with history, with reality, with deadly truth" (76). The point, however, applies to literature as well. How do we establish a balance between a reader reading himself or herself into a text and a text inviting a particular reading that may exclude a reader's particularized experience? If there are no women in Norris's *The Octopus* and the class includes a number of women, do we simply refuse to teach it? Are female students entitled to dismiss it because their "representatives" aren't present in the novel? Aren't these the kinds of questions we all should be asking? Isn't this a variation on Morrison's point about inside and outside cultures? To tease out these questions, I return to my theme: *why might we want students to read literature?* I think, not to become experts. I think, to continue to read, to question, to think reflectively. And I think, yes, like Lori, to see literature as a means of bringing people together: "However, I still believe that literature serves to connect people to each other, rather than to divide us into groups based on our preferences."

Literature is published in multiple media; our courses in literature need to be equally inclusive. As Neil Postman explains, "What we need to consider about the computer has nothing to do with its efficiency as a teaching tool. We need to know in what ways it is altering our conception of learning, and how, in conjunction with television, it undermines the old idea of school" (qtd. in Kaplan). As outlined here, technology, through the lived curriculum, is changing the idea of school, in some ways making school anachronistic. In other ways, school may be not rejuvenated so much as transformed; the multiplicity of media, as Elizabeth Daley suggests, makes new kinds of learning and new texts available. It also underscores a new definition of the student as someone who creates as well as consumes. In the case of literature, this means the creation of literature, as Morrison suggests; the performance of literature of various kinds; both print and digital portfolios; perhaps new pop-up texts that are remediated versions of canonical poetry; reviews of movies and books that situate one in the context of the others. Or—a networked literature course, the purpose of which is to help students begin to create the networks that will sustain them for a lifetime.

Our teaching, too, may be influenced by technology. James Paul Gee makes a strong case for building the principles of gaming into the delivered curriculum. He suggests, for instance, that games are so successful in teaching kids skills because kids are goal oriented: "Learning works best when the learners are so caught up in their goals that they don't realize they are learning or how much they are learning, or when they actively seek new learning inside and outside the game." Likewise, he believes that the ties between informal and formal learning have to count: "Games can allow us to recruit the incredible power of informal learning—the sort of learning that humans are best at—inside formal learning spaces. But real change must happen in these formal learning spaces" ("The Lessons"). *Real change,* then, is what good learning is about. In a general education literature class, what that means, it seems to me, is not only that students read better but also that they choose to read, now *and* when they walk out the door.

These suggestions, then, are an attempt to think about how we might work toward that end.

Practices are constitutive. The practices in these curricula—the lived, the delivered, and the experienced—construct a student who is reading, who is aware of how he or she reads, and who thinks about and reflects on literature, reading processes, and culture in a contrastive mode. The learning, as the teaching, is both by design and by accident.

Our representations of learning—here in this volume, on students' notes, and inside their portfolios—speak to reading practices, which, as philosopher Todd May reminds us, are constitutive in ways we don't always appreciate. Much like Donald Schön (*Educating*) and Lee Schulman, May suggests that what we know and what we hold dear are created through practice. He also understands practice as social and thus ethical. Like the rhetoricians of ancient Greece, May looks to language—to ordered complexity—for the means of helping people move beyond information to understanding, possibly to wisdom.

This project outlines a set of new reading practices. Through such practices, May reminds us, we compose identity, reading by reading, task by rhetorical task, moment by reflective moment.

> It was evening all afternoon
> It was snowing
> And it was going to snow.
> The blackbird sat
> In the cedar-limbs
>
> Wallace Stevens, "Thirteen Ways
> of Looking at a Blackbird"

Notes

1. Another way to talk about the changes that have characterized education in the last quarter-century is to see teaching as shifting from a primarily private activity to a public, shared activity: we see the public in teaching portfolios and in team-teaching; we see the shared in program goal statements that express relationships between multisections of the same course and between courses within a program.

2. Indeed, the very language of the Web assumes that "content" is independent of the medium.

3. This is less true for many nontraditional students, as well as for students of color.

4. Interestingly, "reader's block" is discussed on the Web. The Internet is another site where the lived curriculum plays out; exploring the various kinds of reader's block readers describe would make an interesting study. What is described here, an interruption in a particular kind of reading practice (i.e., of novels), seems radically different from an inability to complete a text because the strategies that would make that possible aren't identified or available.

Bibliography

Adams, Paul C., Steven Hoelscher, and Karen E. Till. "Place in Context: Rethinking Humanist Geographies." In Paul C. Adams, Steven Hoelscher, and Karen E. Till, eds., *Textures of Place: Exploring Humanist Geographies*. Minneapolis: University of Minnesota Press, 2001. viii–xxxiii.

Allen, Michael, Jane Frick, Jeff Sommers, and Kathleen Yancey. "Outside Review of Writing Portfolios: An On-Line Evaluation," *Writing Program Administration* 20.3 (1997): 64–88.

Als, Hilton. "Profiles: Ghosts in the House: Toni Morrison's Writing Life." *New Yorker* (27 Oct. 2003): 64–75.

Applebee, Arthur N. *Curriculum as Conversation: Transforming Traditions of Teaching and Learning*. Chicago: University of Chicago Press, 1996.

Aronson, Anne. "Online Journals: Making the Visible Visual in Academic Writing." English Matters 3. Available at http://chnm.gmu.edu/ematters/issue3/aronson/intro.html (Last accessed 9 Feb. 2004).

Bakhtin, M. M. "Discourse in the Novel." *The Dialogic Imagination: Four Essays*. Michael Holquist, ed. and trans., Caryl Emerson, trans. Austin: University of Texas Press. 259–422.

Barton, Ben F., and Marthalee S. Barton. "Ideology and the Map: Toward a Postmodern Visual Design Practice." In Nancy Roundy Blyler and Charlotte Thralls, eds., *Professional Communication: The Social Perspective*. Newbury Park, CA: Sage, 1993. 49–79.

Bass, Randy. Personal conversation at NCTE Summer Institute, Ocean Creek, 1998.

Bate, W. Jackson. *The Burden of the Past and the English Poet*. Cambridge, MA: Belknap Press, 1970.

Beavis, Catherine. "'It Makes You Realize, Really, Just How Deep Your Subtext Is': Literature, Subjectivity, and Curriculum Change." *Research in the Teaching of English* 36.1 (2001): 38–63.

Birnbaum, June Cannell. "Reflective Thought: The Connection between Reading and Writing." In Bruce T. Peterson, ed., *Convergences: Transactions in Reading and Writing*. Urbana: National Council of Teachers of English, 1986. 30–45.

Bitzer, Lloyd. "The Rhetorical Situation." *Philosophy & Rhetoric* 1.1 (1968): 1–14.

Bloom, Harold. *The Anxiety of Influence: A Theory of Poetry*. New York: Oxford University Press, 1973.

Bolter, Jay David, and Richard Grusin. *Remediation: Understanding New Media*. Cambridge, MA: MIT Press, 2000.

Booth, David. "By Chance and by Design: Incidents of Learning" [Lecture in the series "Putting Interdisciplinary Studies to Work in the World" (or) "Something I Learned in the Paracollege"]. 12 Oct. 1999. Available at www.stolaf.edu/people/booth/incident.html (Last accessed 9 Feb. 2004).

Boyer, Ernest L., and Arthur Levine. *A Quest for Common Learning: The Aims of General Education.* Washington, DC: Carnegie Foundation for the Advancement of Teaching, 1981.

Brandt, Deborah. "Sponsors of Literacy." *College Composition and Communication* 49.2 (May 1998): 165–85.

Brent, Doug. "Rhetorics of the Web: Implications for Teachers of Literacy." Available at www.acs.ucalgary.ca/~dabrent/webliteracies/wayin.htm (Last accessed 9 Feb. 2004).

Brookfield, Stephen D. *Becoming a Critically Reflective Teacher.* San Francisco: Jossey-Bass, 1995.

Cambridge, Barbara L., Susan Kahn, Daniel P. Tompkins, and Kathleen Blake Yancey, eds. *Electronic Portfolios: Emerging Practices in Student, Faculty, and Institutional Learning.* Washington, DC: American Association for Higher Education, 2001.

Cantor, Nancy, and Steven Schomberg. "What We Want Students to Learn: Cultivating Playfulness and Responsibility in a Liberal Education." *Change* 34.6 (November/December 2002). Available at www.oc.uiuc.edu/chancellor/cantorchange.htm (Last accessed 9 Feb. 2004).

Christenbury, Leila. "Afterword: Future Directions for Reading in High School." In Bonnie O. Ericson, ed., *Teaching Reading in High School English Classes.* Urbana, IL: National Council of Teachers of English, 2001. 155–58.

Clark, Gregory. "Genre as Relation: On Writing and Reading as Ethical Interaction." In Wendy Bishop and Hans Ostrom, eds., *Genre and Writing: Issues, Arguments, Alternatives.* Portsmouth, NH: Boynton/Cook-Heinemann, 1997. 125–35.

Daley, Elizabeth M. "Expanding the Concept of Literacy." *Educause Review* 38.2 (March/April 2003): 32–40.

———. "Screen as Vernacular: An Expanding Concept of Literacy." John Seely Brown Lecture, Second John Seely Brown Symposium on Technology and Society, University of Michigan School of Information, Ann Arbor. 3 Oct. 2002. Available at www.si.umich.edu/jsb (Last accessed 2 Mar. 2004).

D'Ambrosio, Charles. "Documents." *New Yorker* (17 June 2002): 71–75.

Davidson, Michael. "Palimtext." In Marjorie Perloff, ed., *Postmodern Genres.* Norman: University of Oklahoma Press, 1989. 75–96.

de Certeau, Michel. *The Practice of Everyday Life.* Berkeley: University of California Press, 1984.

Denby, David. "Creep Shows." *New Yorker* (27 Oct. 2003): 112–13.

Dewey, John. *How We Think: A Restatement of the Relation of Reflective Thinking to the Educative Process.* Boston: D. C. Heath, 1933.

Dickson, Chicksey. Personal e-mail. May 2002.

———. Chicksey Dickson's Summary of Comments from the Director of the Woodrow Wilson Center. WPA-L (Writing Program Administrators listserv), October 2003.

Dirda, Michael. "Sunday." *The Washington Post* (12 Oct. 2003): BW15.

Elbow, Peter. "The Cultures of Literature and Composition: What Could Each Learn from the Other?" *College English* 64.5 (May 2002): 533–46.

———. *Embracing Contraries: Explorations in Learning and Teaching.* New York: Oxford University Press, 1986.

Ellis, Lindsay, Anne Ruggles Gere, and L. Jill Lamberton. "Out Loud: The Common Language of Poetry." *English Journal* 93.1 (September 2003): 44–49.

Flower, Linda S., and John R. Hayes. *A Process Model of Composition.* Pittsburgh, PA: Document Design Project, Carnegie Mellon University, 1979.

Gallagher, Chris W. *Radical Departures: Composition and Progressive Pedagogy.* Urbana, IL: National Council of Teachers of English, 2002.

Gardner, Howard. *Frames of Mind: The Theory of Multiple Intelligences.* New York: Basic Books, 1993.

Gee, James Paul. "The Lessons of Video Games." Colloquy in Print with James Gee. *Chronicle of Higher Education* 50.4 (19 Sept. 2003): B17.

———.*What Video Games Have to Teach Us about Learning and Literacy.* New York: Palgrave Macmillan, 2003.

Gere, Anne Ruggles. "Kitchen Tables and Rented Rooms: The Extracurriculum of Composition." *College Composition and Communication* 45.1 (February 1994): 75–92.

Gioia, Dana. *Can Poetry Matter? Essays on Poetry and American Culture.* St. Paul, MN: Graywolf Press, 2002. Available at Pick of the Litter, Graywolf Press, www.graywolfpress.org/resources/excerpts/ excerpts-canpoetrymatter.html (Last accessed 9 Feb. 2004).

———. "Moulin Rogue: Can Film-maker Baz Luhrman Really Make *La Bohème* Sing for a Broadway Audience?" *San Francisco Magazine,* October 2002. Available at www.danagioia.net/essays/eluhrman.htm (Last accessed 9 Feb. 2004).

Graff , Gerald. Afterword. In Art Young and Toby Fulwiler, eds., *When Writing Teachers Teach Literature: Bringing Writing to Reading.* Portsmouth, NH: Boynton/Cook, 1995. 324–34.

———. "Hidden Intellectualism." *Pedagogy* 1.1 (2001): 21–36.

Guillory, John. "The Very Idea of Pedagogy." *Profession 2002.* New York: MLA. 164–71.

Hillocks, George Jr. *Teaching Writing as Reflective Practice*. New York: Teachers College Press, 1995.

Hirsch, Edward. In Contributors Notes and Comments. In Yusef Komunyakaa and David Lehman, eds., *The Best American Poetry, 2003*. New York: Scribner, 2003.

hooks, bell. *Talking Back: Thinking Feminist, Thinking Black*. Boston: South End Press, 1989.

Hult, Christine. "Using Online Portfolios to Assess English Majors at Utah State University." In Barbara L. Cambridge, Susan Kahn, Daniel P. Tompkins, and Kathleen Blake Yancey, eds., *Electronic Portfolios: Emerging Practices in Student, Faculty, and Institutional Learning*. Washington, DC: American Association for Higher Education, 2001. 71–76.

Jdroth. "Reader's Block" [Foldedspace blog]. 15 Oct. 2003. Available at www.foldedspace.org/archives/000858.html (Last accessed 2 Mar. 2004).

Kaplan, Nancy. "What Neil Postman Has to Say." *Computer-Mediated Communication Magazine* 2.3 (1 Mar. 1995): 34. Available at www.ibiblio.org/cmc/mag/1995/mar/hyper/npcontexts_119.html (Last accessed 2 Mar. 2004).

Kettel, Raymond P., and Nancy L. Douglas. "Comprehending Multiple Texts: A Theme Approach to Incorporating the Best of Children's Literature." *Voices from the Middle* 11.1 (Sept. 2003): 43–49. Available at www.soe.umd.umich.edu/rpkettel/VM0111Comprehending.pdf (Last accessed 11 Feb. 2003).

Kremer, Belinda. "So It Was This Beautiful Night." In Christopher Schroeder, Helen Fox, and Patricia Bizzell, eds., *ALT DIS: Alternative Discourses and the Academy*. Portsmouth: Boynton/Cook, 2002. 97–112.

Komunyakaa, Yusef. Introduction. In Yusef Komunyakaa and David Lehman, eds., *The Best of American Poetry, 2003*. New York: Scribner, 2003. 11–21.

Kress, Gunther. "Design and Transformation: New Theories of Meaning." In Bill Cope and Mary Kalantzis, eds., *Multiliteracies: Literacy Learning and the Design of Social Futures*. New York: Routledge, 2000. 153–62.

Langer, Judith A. *Effective Literacy Instruction: Building Successful Reading and Writing Programs*. Urbana, IL: National Council of Teachers of English, 2002.

Lanham, Richard A. *The Electronic Word: Democracy, Technology, and the Arts*. Chicago: University of Chicago Press, 1993.

Light, Richard J. *Making the Most of College: Students Speak Their Minds*. Cambridge, MA: Harvard University Press, 2001.

Lloyd-Jones, Richard, and Andrea A. Lunsford, eds. *The English Coalition Conference: Democracy through Language*. Urbana, IL: National Council of Teachers of English, and New York: Modern Language Association, 1989.

Mac. In Trackback Comments to "Reader's Block" [Foldedspace blog]. 16 Oct. 2003 08:17 a.m. Available at www.foldedspace.org/archives/ 000858.html (Last accessed 2 Mar. 2004).

May, Todd. *Our Practices, Our Selves, or, What It Means to Be Human*. University Park: Penn State University Press, 2001.

Mayher, John S. *Uncommon Sense: Theoretical Practice in Language Education*. Portsmouth, NH: Boynton/Cook, 1990.

McCormick, Kathleen. *The Culture of Reading and the Teaching of English*. Manchester, UK: Manchester University Press, 1994.

McGann, Jerome, et al. "'Reading Fiction/Teaching Fiction': A Pedagogical Experiment." *Pedagogy* 1.1 (2000): 143–65.

McLuhan, Marshall, and Quentin Fiore. *The Medium Is the Massage: An Inventory of Effects*. 1967. Corte Madera, CA: Gingko, 2001.

Miller, Richard E. *As If Learning Mattered: Reforming Higher Education*. Ithaca, NY: Cornell University Press, 1998.

MLA Ad Hoc Committee on the Professionalization of PhDs. "Professionalization in Perspective." *Profession 2002*. New York: MLA. 187–210.

Moffett, James. *Teaching the Universe of Discourse*. Portsmouth, NH: Boynton/ Cook, 1987.

Moran, Karen, and Jennifer E. Carson. "Conversation Sparks: How to Jumpstart Comprehension." *Voices from the Middle* 11.1 (September 2003): 29–30.

Ochs, Elinor, and Lisa Capps. *Living Narrative: Creating Lives in Everyday Storytelling*. Cambridge, MA: Harvard University Press, 2001.

Ozick, Cynthia. "Who Owns Anne Frank?" *The New Yorker* (6 Oct. 1997): 76–87.

Peterson, Beverly. "Inviting Students to Challenge the American Literature Syllabus." *Teaching English in the Two-Year College* 28.4 (May 2001): 379–82.

Purves, Alan. "Telling Our Story about Teaching Literature." *Profession 1997*. New York: MLA. 52–61.

Ramsay, John G. "Hell's Bibliophiles: The Fifth Way of Looking at an Aliterate." *Change* 34.1 (January-February, 2002): 50–56.

Roen, Duane. Rev. of *A Guide to Composition Pedagogies*, ed. Gary Tate, Amy Rupiper, and Kurt Schick. *Rhetoric Review* 21 (2002): 114–17.

Rosenblatt, Louise M. *The Reader, the Text, the Poem*. Carbondale: Southern Illinois University Press, 1994.

Schank, Roger. Back to Basics Problems. *Engines for Education*. Available at www.engines4ed.org/hyperbook/nodes/NODE-74-pg.html (Last accessed 9 Feb. 2004).

Scholes, Robert. *The Rise and Fall of English: Reconstructing English as a Discipline.* New Haven: Yale University Press, 1998.

———. *Textual Power: Literary Theory and the Teaching of English.* New Haven: Yale University Press, 1985.

———. "The Transition to College Reading." *Pedagogy* 2.2 (2002): 165–72.

Schön, Donald A. "Causality and Causal Inference in the Study of Organizations." In Robert F. Goodman and Walter R. Fisher, eds., *Rethinking Knowledge: Reflections across the Disciplines.* Albany: SUNY Press, 1995. 69–103.

———. *Educating the Reflective Practitioner: Toward a New Design for Teaching and Learning in the Professions.* San Francisco: Jossey-Bass, 1987.

Schulman, Lee. "Making Differences: A Table of Learning." *Change* 34.6 (November/December 2002). Available at www.carnegiefoundation. org/elibrary/docs/making_differences.htm (Last accessed 9 Feb. 2004).

Schuster, Charles. "Teaching Literature through Performance." In Art Young and Toby Fulwiler, eds., *When Writing Teachers Teach Literature: Bringing Writing to Reading.* Portsmouth, NH: Boynton/Cook, 1995. 135–47.

Schwalm, David. "Re: Large Lecture." Online posting. 6 Oct. 2003. Writing Program Administrators listserv (WPA-L) (Last accessed 13 May 2004).

Sellen, Abigail J., and Richard H. R. Harper. *The Myth of the Paperless Office.* Cambridge, MA: MIT Press, 2001.

Sirc, Geoffrey. *English Composition as a Happening.* Logan: Utah State University Press, 2002.

Slevin, James F. "Keeping the University Occupied and out of Trouble." *Profession 2002.* New York: MLA. 63–71.

Sommers, Jeff. "Portfolios in Literature Courses: A Case Study." *Teaching English in the Two-Year College* 24.3 (October 1997): 220–34.

Stevens, Wallace. "Thirteen Ways of Looking at a Blackbird." *Harmonium* (7 Sept. 1923): 135–37. Rpt. on *Representative Poetry Online,* http:// eir.library.utoronto.ca/rpo/display/poem2018.html (Last accessed 2 Mar. 2004).

Summerfield, Judith, and Geoffrey Summerfield. *Frames of Mind: A Course in Composition.* New York: Random House, 1986.

Tinburg, Howard. "Starting Where Students Are, but Knowing (and Letting Them Know) Where We Want to Take Them" [Editorial]. *Teaching English in the Two-Year College* 30.1 (Sept. 2002): 5.

van Bruggen, Coosje. *Frank O. Gehry: Guggenheim Museum Bilbao.* New York: Guggenheim Museum Publications, 1999.

Vygotsky, L. S. *Mind in Society: The Development of Higher Psychological Processes.* Cambridge, MA: Harvard University Press, 1978.

———. *Thought and Language.* Ed. and trans. Eugenia Hanfmann and Gertrude Vakar. Cambridge, MA: MIT Press, 1962.

Wickliff, Greg, and Kathleen Blake Yancey. "The Perils of Creating a Class Web Site: It Was the Best of Times, It Was the . . . ." *Computers and Composition* 18.2 (2001): 177–86.

Winch, Terrence. "My Work." In Yusef Komunyakaa and David Lehman, eds., *The Best American Poetry, 2003.* New York: Scribner, 2003. 180–82.

Yancey, Kathleen Blake. "The Plural Commons: Meeting the Future of English Studies." In Robert P. Yagelski and Scott A. Leonard, eds., *The Relevance of English: Teaching That Matters in Students' Lives.* Urbana, IL: National Council of Teachers of English, 2002. 382–400.

———. *Reflection in the Writing Classroom.* Logan: Utah State University Press, 1998.

———. "Teacher Portfolios: Lessons on Resistance, Readiness, and Reflection." In Kathleen Blake Yancey and Irwin Weiser, eds., *Situating Portfolios: Four Perspectives.* Logan: Utah State University Press, 1997. 244–63.

Yardley, Jonathan. "State of the Art." *Washington Post* 14 July 2002. Available at www.washingtonpost.com/ac2/wp-dyn/A57255-2002Jul11?language=printer (Last accessed 9 Feb. 2004).

Young, Art, and Toby Fulwiler, eds. *When Writing Teachers Teach Literature: Bringing Writing to Reading.* Portsmouth, NH: Boynton/Cook, 1995.

Young, Richard. "Arts, Crafts, Gifts, and Knacks." In Aviva Freedman and Ian Pringle, eds., *Reinventing the Rhetorical Tradition.* Ontario: Canadian Council of Teachers of English, and Conway, AR: L&S Books, University of Central Arkansas, 1980. 53–60.

Index

Author

Kathleen Blake Yancey is R. Roy Pearce Professor of Professional Communication at Clemson University, where in addition to directing the Pearce Center and its Student Studio, she teaches classes in writing and in literature. She is past chair of the College Section of NCTE, past co-director of the UNC Charlotte site of the National Writing Project, and current chair of the Conference on College Composition and Communication. Author of more than forty articles and book chapters and author or editor of seven volumes, Yancey here considers what the purposes for a literature course for general education should be, and she connects these purposes to reflective practice more generally. Like her work in *Situating Portfolios* and *Reflection in the Writing Classroom*, this new curriculum for literature looks to reflection as a means of learning for both students and teachers.

*This book was typeset in Palatino, Avant Garde, and Helvetica
by Electronic Imaging.
The typeface used on the cover was EllingtonMT Regular.
The book was printed on 60-lb. Accent Opaque Offset paper by Versa Press.*